南　京　不　会　忘　记

NANJING WILL NEVER FORGET

南京出版传媒集团
南京出版社

约翰·摩尔·阿利森

JOHN MOORE ALLISON

卢彦名　著

图书在版编目（CIP）数据

约翰·摩尔·阿利森 / 卢彦名著. -- 南京：南京出版社，2016.12

（南京不会忘记）

ISBN 978-7-5533-1568-3

Ⅰ. ①约… Ⅱ. ①卢… Ⅲ. ①约翰·摩尔·阿利森 - 生平事迹 Ⅳ. ①K837.127=5

中国版本图书馆CIP数据核字（2016）第279420号

丛 书 名：南京不会忘记
书 名：约翰·摩尔·阿利森
作 者：卢彦名
出版发行：南京出版传媒集团
南 京 出 版 社

社址：南京市太平门街53号 邮编：210016
网址：http://www.njcbs.cn 电子信箱：njcbs1988@163.com
淘宝网店：http://njpress.taobao.com 天猫网店：http://njcbcmjtts.tmall.com
联系电话：025-83283893、83283864（营销） 025-83112257（编务）

出 版 人：朱同芳
出 品 人：卢海鸣
责任编辑：林莉萍
装帧设计：朱赢椿 杨杰芳
责任印制：杨福彬

排 版：南京新华丰制版有限公司
印 刷：南京玉河印刷厂
开 本：787毫米 × 1092毫米 1/32
印 张：3.875
字 数：63千
版 次：2016 年12月第 1 版
印 次：2016 年12月第 1 次印刷
书 号：ISBN 978-7-5533-1568-3
定 价：15.00 元

淘宝网店 天猫网店

编委会

总 序　PREFACE

如果说，一个惨痛的事件近80年来一直被人们铭记，那是因为我们拒绝这样的事件再次发生。1937年12月13日，南京沦陷。日军侵占南京后在短短数周内屠杀放下武器的中国士兵和平民超过30万之众，超过两万名妇女被强奸，无数的公私财物遭到破坏。南京大屠杀成为南京这座城市的痛史，也成为全世界、全人类的一页痛史。

如果说，一些人在时光流逝了近80年后，一直没有被忘怀，那是因为他们在灾难面前表现出悲天悯人的情怀。在南京大屠杀的血雨腥风里，一批国际义士以担当、坚守与抗争诠释了人性的光辉。他们设立国际安全区，竭尽所能保护了20多万难民。

正如金陵女子文理学院美籍教授魏特琳曾在日记中记载："我觉得我在金陵女子文理学院18年的经历，以及与邻居14年的交往经验，使我能够担负起一些责任，这也是我的使命，就像在危险之中，男人们不应弃船而去，女人也不应丢弃她们的孩子一样。"而当时留在南京的美国人乔治·费奇也曾经说过："我生于中国，半生服务又在中国，所以中国已成为我的第二故乡。我在中国服务，也是在为我的祖国服务，同时也是为人类正义与民主和平而服务。"

滴水之恩，当涌泉相报。中国人民没有忘记这些国际义士。2014 年 12 月 13 日，习近平总书记在首次南京大屠杀死难者国家公祭仪式上说：“令人感动的是，在南京大屠杀那些腥风血雨的日子里，我们的同胞守望相助、相互支持，众多国际友人也冒着风险，以各种方式保护南京民众，并记录下日本侵略者的残暴行径。他们中有德国的约翰·拉贝、丹麦的贝恩哈尔·辛德贝格、美国的约翰·马吉等人。对他们的人道精神和无畏义举，中国人民永远不会忘记。”

在第三个南京大屠杀死难者国家公祭日来临之际，侵华日军南京大屠杀遇难同胞纪念馆、南京出版社组织专家编撰出版了“南京不会忘记”丛书。丛书采用第三方人士的独特视角，借助大量的中、美、德等国的原始文献、书信、日记，再现了国际义士们的勇敢和大义。相信此套丛书的出版，不仅仅是单纯讲述历史，更是为了记住在黑暗中的人性光芒，在人间炼狱中的一抹温暖。

让我们铭记：美国人约翰·马吉、乔治·费奇、明妮·魏特琳、米讷·舍尔·贝德士、罗伯特·威尔逊、刘易斯·史迈士、米尔士、特里默、格瑞斯·鲍尔、伊娃·海因兹、麦卡伦、休伯特·索恩、欧内斯特·福斯特、里格斯、约翰·摩尔·阿利森、埃斯皮、麦克法恩、阿契包德·斯蒂尔、弗兰克·德丁、查尔斯·麦克丹尼尔、阿瑟·孟肯，德国人约翰·拉贝、克勒格尔、曹迪希、黑姆佩尔、爱德华·施佩林、卡尔·京特、格奥尔格·罗森、许尔特尔、沙尔芬贝格，丹麦人贝恩哈尔·阿尔普·辛德贝格，英国人莱利斯·史密斯，奥地利人哈茨，白俄人波德希沃洛夫、齐阿尔……

南京不会忘记！

中共江苏省委常委、宣传部部长　王燕文

引 言 FOREWORD

侵华日军南京大屠杀期间留守南京的美籍人士，以及大屠杀后返回南京的美国外交官，利用特殊的身份，在目睹、收集、调查和抗议侵华日军对在南京的美国财产和人员侵犯情况的同时，还调查和揭露了侵华日军在南京犯下的烧、杀、淫、掠暴行，并留下了大量第一手的文献档案资料和外交文件。在这其中，时任美国驻南京大使馆二等秘书的约翰·摩尔·阿利森（John Moore Allison）是身份非常特殊的一位人士。这位长期游走于中国和日本之间的美国资深外交官，为我们了解南京大屠杀提供了一个独特的视角。

南京的沦陷，对身处战火中的人来说，无疑是生死转瞬的极端状态。在近代中国的大背景中，战争似乎比和平更为寻常，尤其对相对超脱于战火之外的西方人士来说更是如此。日军在南京大屠杀前后不仅对中国人大肆施暴，而且广泛地侵害了第三方的权益，并引起了相关受害者与日方十分频繁地在多层次的交涉。可以说，南京大屠杀是一场涉及多国的国际暴行。在此期间，以阿利森为代表的西方外交官群体，以忠实履行外交官职责的方式，在努力制止侵华日军暴行的同时，沟通中国大众和中美高层，推动了中美之间的互动，从而在宏观政策上以及中美两国关系中发挥了重要作用，例如推动美国对日本的武器禁售决定。他们的活动不仅对当时的中国，而且对战争局势以及东亚秩序都产生了深远的影响。

侵华日军南京大屠杀虽然事发于中华民国的首都南京，然而中文资料却相对零散，且直接相关者多为回忆等事后形成的资料，在讨论问题时有效性和准确性都有所欠缺。与之相对的是，人数很少的西方人士却在第一时间形成了大量的文字材料。南京大屠杀期间返回南京的美、英、德等国外交人士形成的外交档案，其价值更是不言而喻。

目 录 CONTENTS

001 早年生涯

011 驻华外交官

023 临危受命

039 再抵南京

061 “阿利森事件”

075 不辱使命

091 余生浮沉

104 主要参考资料

约翰·摩尔·阿利森 John Moore Allison

早年生涯

位于黄浦路 13—14 号的美国驻上海总领事馆旧址

约翰·摩尔·阿利森于1905年4月7日出生在美国堪萨斯州的小镇霍顿（Holton），是他的父亲奥斯卡·约翰·阿利森（Oscar John Allison）与母亲安妮B.摩尔·阿利森（Annie B. Moore Allison）的独生子。他的父亲从事火炉经销、维修的生意，在小阿利森年幼时便举家迁往内布拉斯加州的首府林肯市。阿利森在林肯长大、就学，1922年从林肯高级中学毕业后进入内布拉斯加大学，主修政治学，辅修英文。内布拉斯加大学林肯分校是美国中西部久负盛名的公立综合性大学，因教学严谨被誉为公立常青藤学校。美国著名军事家，特级上将（级别高于五星上将）约翰·约瑟夫·潘兴（John Joseph Pershing，1860—1948）就毕业于该校的法学院。巧合的是，作为青年阿利森的老学长和偶像，潘兴曾经在日俄战争期间担任美国驻日本武官。而阿利森后来也长期担任驻日本外交官。这两位内布拉斯加大学的杰出毕业生以这样一种特殊的方式产生了交集。

阿利森在内布拉斯加大学就读二年级时，偶然结识了一位朋友。这个人名叫亚瑟·约金森（Arthur Jorgensen）。约金森多年前毕业于内布拉斯加大学，曾在日本的基督教青年会（YMCA）工作了15年。此时，他已经回到母校主持内布拉斯加大学基督教青年会的工作。与约金森的交往对阿利森往后的生活道路产生了深远的影响，约金森的生动描绘使得年轻的阿利森对遥远而神秘的东方产生了浓厚的兴趣。许多年以后，阿利森在他的回忆录里写道："出于某种原因，我一直向往能够去亚洲，而不是欧洲。"在约金森的鼓励下，阿利森决定去日本教英文。1927 年 6 月，刚刚大学毕业的阿利森在基督教青年会的推荐安排下踏上了前往日本的路程。

阿利森在日本待了两年，先在神奈川县的小田原中学、厚木中学两所学校教英文，以后于 1928 年 4 月前往位于京都舞鹤地区的日本海军机关学校教英语。在当时，海军机关学校与海军兵学校、海军经理学校是旧日本帝国海军三大学校，是日本海军军官的摇篮之一。例如，号称日本飞机大王的军需康采恩头目中岛知久平（1884—1949）就毕业于该校。后来参加进攻南京作战的日本海军舰队中的许多军官，也有很多是毕业于海军机关学校。在日本的早年游历使阿利森对日本社会有了深入的了解和敏锐的洞悉。此时的阿利森或许不会想到，若干年之后，在远东另一个国家的土地上，他将会与这些他所熟悉的日本军人展开坚决的斗争。1938 年 1 月，当阿利森乘坐美舰"瓦胡"号在南京附近的江面进退维谷的时候，拦阻在他面前的正是他昔日在日本海军机关学校的同事和学生们。最后，阿利森也将成为目睹美日关系逐步恶化乃至兵戎相见的见证人。

一次偶然的机会，阿利森在火车上和一位美国商人相遇。闲谈之余，这位商人介绍阿利森去上海工作。于是，阿利森在1929年6月成为美国通用汽车公司上海分公司的推销经理。在上海，阿利森结识了不少朋友，其中有后来大名鼎鼎的美国记者埃德加·斯诺以及同情中国革命的爱格妮丝·史沫特莱。

20世纪20年代末并不是个从商的好年头。大萧条的到来断送了无数人从商谋生的前程。但阿利森幸运地

1929年阿利森在上海美国通用公司

结识了一位来自内布拉斯加州奥马哈的老乡亚瑟·林沃特（Arthur Ringwalt）。林沃特当时在美国驻上海总领事馆任副领事。眼看着阿利森就要失业的时候，林沃特在1930年4月把阿利森介绍进了上海总领事馆，在商务处做个职员。由此，阿利森开始了他的外交官生涯。

1930年10月正式通过美国国务院的外交人员资格考试之后，阿利森晋升为副领事，被派往驻日本神户领事馆工作。为了更好地学习掌握日语，他在1932年2月到驻东京大使馆参加为期两年的强化学习日本语言、历史和文化的训练班，大大提高了他的日语能力。这为他日后的外交生涯，直至在战后成为美国驻日本大使奠定了坚实的基础。

位于黄浦路13—14号的美国驻上海总领事馆旧址

1932 年，阿利森出任美国驻日本神户副领事。此时，美日外交关系正发生着微妙的变化。1931 年，日本侵略中国东北，对维持太平洋均势的条约体系（1922 年的《九国公约》和 1928 年的《巴黎非战公约》）提出了严重挑战，日本开始了它的独占政策来取代美国的门户开放政策的武力征服过程。当时担任美国总统的胡佛，正被国内的经济危机弄得焦头烂额，他对主张对日本持较强硬态度的国务卿史汀生所提出的经济制裁建议，一概加以拒绝，只同意发表一个表明美国立场的声明，这就是美国政府在 1932 年 1 月 7 日以致中日两国政府照会的形式发表的政策声明：不承认有损于美国在华条约权利——门户开放政策的任何条约。1933 年 3 月 4 日，富兰克林·罗斯福继胡佛任美国总统。他接受史汀生的“不承认主义”的原则，支持国际条约的“神圣义务”。这一年的 3 月 27 日，日本示威性地退出了国际联盟，声称日本“在建立远东持久和平所应遵循的原则上与国际联盟不合”。

与此同时，美国国内孤立主义盛行。1934 年，美国参议院外委会成立以奈伊为主席的军火调查委员会，该委员会认为“上次参战，我们的目标半点也没有达到”，从而开始了有关中立法的大辩论。在意大利入侵阿比西尼亚（今埃塞俄比亚）前夕，美国国会于 8 月 31 日通过并由罗斯福签署了第一个中立法案，宣布：“凡由美国或美国其他属地之任何地点，将武器、弹药及作战工具输往交战国港口，或输往任何中立国港口以便转运至交战国或为交战国所用均属非法。”这一法案有效期到1936年2月29日。它是在孤立主义影响下通过的。罗斯福在签署时说：“这是表明美国政府及人民避免从事可能使美国卷入战争行运之愿望，但是它可能将使美国卷入战争而不是置身局外。”实际上，1935年的《中立法》是有利于德、意、日法西斯的。在日本神户担任副领事的阿利森此时虽然不在外交部门的核心层，但正默默观

1932年圣诞节，阿利森好友埃德加·斯诺（右）与海伦·福斯特（左）在东京大使馆结婚，阿利森主持了婚礼

察着事态的发展。此时，对日本军国主义扩张政策的担忧和憎恶已经渐渐深埋于阿利森的心中。

1932 年圣诞节，阿利森为好友埃德加·斯诺（Edgar Snow）与海伦·福斯特（Helen Foster）操办婚礼。阿利森本人做伴郎，并说服一位在东京的美国学校教授法语的女郎玛丽·珍妮特·布鲁克斯（Marie Jeanette Brooks）做伴娘。斯诺夫人海伦在回忆录里写道："我不顾许多麻烦，坚持要在圣诞节的正午在东京的美国使馆结婚，由未来的大使约翰·阿利森和他的未婚妻珍妮特作证婚人。"斯诺夫人此前也曾任职于美国驻沪领事馆，和阿利森是同事，不久她辞职成了自由撰稿人。6 个月后的 1933 年 6 月，阿利森与斯诺夫妇那场婚礼的伴娘布鲁克斯小姐也终成眷属。

驻华外交官

日军轰炸后的南京街市

1935年11月，阿利森晋升为领事，被派往美国驻大连领事馆。

阿利森到大连赴任的时候，面临的是错综复杂的政治形势。“九一八”事变后，发动事变的日本关东军为了长期统治中国东北，派遣奉天特务机关长土肥原贤二在天津策动“便衣队暴动”，将隐居于天津的清朝末代皇帝溥仪带到长春，拥立为“满洲国”执政，宣示这个伪政权正式建立。在伪满成立的1932年3月，其“外交总长”谢介石便向日、美、英、法、德、意、苏等17个国家发出通告，希望建立外交关系。但除了日本于6月宣布承认伪满外，其他国家都没有积极回应。美国更在此前发表声明，宣布不承认任何违反《国际联盟盟约》和《巴黎公约》的行为。

由于现实需要的考虑，在伪满政权建立后，欧美各国普遍保留原驻中国东北的领事馆。阿利森抵达大连后，便与前任美国驻大连领事范宣德（John Carter Vincent）进行了商谈。两人一致认为，美国不必担心远东贸易额下降的问题，更不必急于承认伪满洲国。于是，美国外交官就开始了与日本当局的周旋。一方面，阿利森需要保护美国人在满洲的财产和利益；另一方面，他又要避免因拒绝与伪满发生官方联系而激怒日本当局。练就这种在钢丝绳上跳舞的技巧将为日后阿利森在更高层面的外交舞台上的纵横捭阖打下坚实的基础。

1936 年 7 月，阿利森又奉调至驻济南领事馆。

美国势力进入济南较早，但主要是进行传教活动。1905 年以前，美国基督教长老会在济南东关租赁民房，办学传教，如于 1893 年修建济美学馆等。后来，基督教天主会和青年会也先后到来，天主会修建了洪楼大教堂。虽然如此，但是美国侨民数量很少，商业洋行也只有美孚一家，主营石油。鉴于领事馆的目的在于管理侨民，推行商务，似乎美国没有必要在济南设立领事馆。但是美国十分看中济南的地理位置和政治地位，遂于 1918 年 10 月正式建立了领事馆，设领事、副领事各一人，书记、翻译各两人，打字员一人。1921 年 3 月，第三任领事高斯请求建立固定馆舍，得到同意后，美方与济南比商义公司签订契约，按照其要求图样在经七小纬二路东南角建造完成。阿利森来到济南就任时，美国领事馆就坐落于此。

美国驻济南领事馆的主要工作在于情报的搜集。每月 7 日之前，必须要有一份完整的报告，内容涉及政治、经济、军事、商业等各个方面。尤其是必须报告的军政界高级官吏的名单和简历。这些情报的来源，主要是当

济南美国领事馆旧址

地的报纸，山东各县的美国教会、美国商人和中国官吏。所以领事馆设立之初就将济南领事馆的管辖范围界定在胶莱河以西的山东全境，后来为了进一步突出政治功能，将河南省的许多县市的事务也划归为济南领事馆管辖。

1937年7月，日本以制造卢沟桥事变为衅端，发动了全面侵华战争。月底占领北平、天津地区以后，即以30万兵力向华北发动大规模战略进攻。8月13日，日军又大举进攻上海，企图胁迫中国政府订立城下之盟。1937年9月下旬，日军侵华战争由平津南移，直逼黄河。日军离济南城不远之际，阿利森奉命关闭领事馆，撤往南京。此时，阿利森被晋升为大使馆三等秘书，他在南京待到 11 月。

早在 1937 年 8 月 15 日，即淞沪会战的第三天，日军战机便开始对南京实施大轰炸。凄厉的空袭警报声响彻全城，日军海军航空兵开始对南京进行轰炸。轰炸次数越来越频繁，南京城硝烟弥漫。阿利森到达南京时，正是日军轰炸逐渐进入高峰的时期。

从 9 月中旬至 11 月初，日本海军航空队集中优势兵力对南京实施大规模空袭行动。9 月中旬，原驻中国东北周水子机场的日本海军第 2 联合航空队奉命到上海参战，进驻上海日商公大纱厂内抢建的前进机场。该部队准备了当时世界上最先进的九六式舰上战斗机 24 架。同时，日本陆军第 3 飞行团 40 多架飞机也到达上海前线

日军轰炸后的南京街市

支援地面作战，让海军航空队可以集中力量空袭南京等地。9月19日，指挥侵略华东地区的日本海军第3舰队中将司令长官长谷川清在上海发出通告，要求各国驻华使馆将在南京的人员及侨民转移至“安全地区”，各国舰船撤离南京江面，

"All the News That's Fit to Print."

The Ne

VOL. LXXXVII....No. 29,096.

AIR RAIDERS BOMB NANKING AFTER ANGLO-U. S. PROTEST ON PLAN TO DEVASTATE CITY

ATTACK IS TERRIFIC

Lasts Hour and a Half as Thousands Rush to Bomb-Proof Shelters

HALF OF POPULACE FLED

U. S. Ambassador Johnson on Gunboat Stays at Nanking—Other Foreigners on Ships

U. S., BRITAIN SENT APPEAL

In Separate Moves They Urged Japan Not to Bomb a City With Many Noncombatants

By The Associated Press.

NANKING, Wednesday, Sept. 22—Japanese air raiders launched their threatened attack to annihilate Nanking today and bombed this Chinese capital for an hour and a half. The Japanese planes swooped over the city at 10:35 A. M. and the "all clear" was not sounded until noon.

The bombardment was terrific. The blasts from the deadly bombs mingled with the sharp bark of anti-aircraft guns emplaced on the hills about the city. One anti-aircraft shell exploded near the residence of Nelson T. Johnson, the United States Ambassador, who had transferred his staff to United States gunboats in the Yangtze.

Thousands Flee to Shelters

By F. TILLMAN DURDIN

Wireless to THE NEW YORK TIMES.

The Warfare in China

Japanese planes staged a terrific attack on Nanking, bombing the Chinese capital for an hour and a half. Sirens announcing the approach of the aerial armada had sent the populace scurrying to bombproof shelter. The United States Embassy staff was still quartered on a gunboat offshore in the Yangtze River. [Page 1.]

The Japanese threat to bomb Nanking caused both the United States and Great Britain to make representations. The United States took double-barreled action: the Ambassador in Tokyo addressed the Japanese Foreign Office, and the State Department in Washington explained its attitude to the Japanese Ambassador there. [Page 10.] London's representations, made simultaneously but separately, were based on the same broad ground that had underlain the protest against the recent shooting of the British Ambassador in China, that is, that no nation has any right to attack combatants and noncombatants indiscriminately. [Follows the above.] There were reports at Shanghai, apparently caused by the American and British steps, that a joint protest against a bombing of Nanking would be made by all the major powers. [Follows the above.]

Geneva swung slowly into action. The Advisory Committee, with the United States represented, began consideration of the Far Eastern conflict and much seemed to depend on what attitude this country would take. [Page 11.]

On China's war fronts the Japanese battled their way nearer to Paoting and asserted they were now only two miles away from the fortified line of the Chinese some ten miles north of that city [Page 10], while in the south their planes staged two raids on Canton, but were frustrated by Chinese forts and air fighters. [Page 11.]

ITALY JOINS TALKS ON PATROL ROUTES

Accepts Anglo-French Proposal for Parley of Naval Experts to Consider Nyon Changes

ADHERENCE LATER IS SEEN

Rome's Honor Is Satisfied by

FUSION HEADS BAR SUPPORT OF HARVEY

Party Chiefs Refuse to Follow Mayor in Endorsement of Queens President

AGREE ON REST OF TICKET

But Miner Nominations Lag as

1937年9月22日《纽约时报》：不顾英美抗议 日军企图对南京实施毁灭性轰炸

日机将于9月21正午以后对南京城内及附近的中国军队、一切属于军事工作及活动的建筑，采取轰炸及其他手段。其实，日本海军航空队于当天就提前行动了，前后出动了飞机77架次，分两批空袭大校场机场、南京金陵兵工厂、警备司令部、宪兵司令部及许多平民区，市民伤亡百余人。此后至9月25日止的一周内，日本海军

航空队对南京连日轰炸。最多的9月25日达四批，共计动用飞机289架次，投弹总量355枚，计32.3吨。

早在阿利森到达南京之前，在各国使馆的组织下，南京的外国侨民已经开始分批撤离这个“每小时都会遭到轰炸”的危险之地。1937年8月16日，美国大使馆建议侨民将所有的妇女和儿童转移到比较安全的庐山牯岭或者汉口。9月抵达南京的阿利森也积极参与到了这项转移行动的组织中。

1937年8月，英国驻华大使许阁森乘坐以大幅英国国旗标明的汽车前往上海途中，遭到日军飞机故意袭击，车辆倾覆，许阁森身受重伤。许阁森被日本空军所伤，躺在上海的医院里，然而英国驻华使馆代办豪（R.G.Howe）决定坚守在南京他的岗位上。这使得美国大使詹森（Nelson Frusler Johnson）对执行美国政府最近给美国使馆、公使馆和领事馆下发的“标准”命令有些犹豫不决，这些命令要求在现地的高级官员根据自己的判断决定什么对他本人及使馆成员构成“不必要的冒险”。詹森大使对美联社说：“我非常悲伤，难以表述，这是我30年的职业生涯中第一次被迫离开自己的岗位……我不能够拿我们使馆的忠实的工作人员的性命冒险，我不是逃兵。”当詹森大使及使馆工作人员转移到停靠在南京江边的“吕宋”号和“关岛”号炮艇上的消息迅速传到中国外交部的时候，美国使馆的二等秘书帕克斯顿（J.Hall Paxton），独自提出他是否可以留在南京，以便使美国大使馆继续开放。大使的回答是“可以”。

值得一提的是，当时在南京的还有一批身份特殊的美国人，那就是以陈纳德和小比利·麦克唐纳为首的美籍军事顾问。1937 年，全面抗战爆发之前，陈纳德将军已应蒋介石之邀来到中国，但蒋介石一开始只让他以观察员身份制定空战的计划，指导中国空军的对日作战。抗日战争爆发后，他当即表示：“如有需要，愿意尽力为中国服务。”陈纳德当时不仅做教官，还担任了中国

美籍空军顾问鲁克·威廉姆森（穿大衣者）等在机场检阅

空军一个中队的队长，他带领这支中队在保卫南京上空的时候，与日军作战。阿利森与陈纳德将军的初次相识就在战火中的南京。

到了 11 月的时候，由于日军暂时还没有侵占济南，时任美国驻华大使詹森同意阿利森返回济南。但是，阿利森刚刚抵达济南没有几天，形势骤变。日军正积极准备渡过黄河，济南已经危在旦夕。阿利森接到美国国务院的指示，要他经青岛、上海，再次撤往南京。

11 月底，阿利森抵达上海之际，战事已临近南京。1937 年 11 月，日军攻占上海之后，节节向南京进逼。国民政府于 11 月 20 日宣布将首都迁往重庆，但是蒋介石和外交部、财政部、交通部等国民政府的中枢机构暂

1937 年的美国大使馆(1937 年9月22号拍摄)

美国大使詹森（左三）等在金陵大学考察

时迁往汉口办公。各国驻华使节，包括美国驻中国大使詹森与大使馆的大部分工作人员，也随之迁往汉口，在南京只留下极少数外交官坚守到日军总攻之前。12月10日，在南京留有外交人员的美、英、德三国使馆的所有留守外交官均登上英美炮艇或商船撤离。詹森离开南京后，根据其指示，美驻上海总领事高斯（Clarence Edward Gauss）将南京有关情况通知了上海的日本当局，并表示："大使馆要求日本军事当局及民事当局注意上述描述的情况，如果出现需要，充分地承认大使馆工作人员及使馆的外交地位，并给予他们适当的便利和完全

南京沦陷前夕，美国大使馆留守外交官员在所有美国人的房产上张贴了由大使馆和南京卫戍司令部发布的公告

的保护。”美国大使馆留守外交官员在南京沦陷前夕撤离时，在所有美国人的房产上张贴了由大使馆和卫戍司令部发布的公告，并且给留下来看管美国使馆财产的仆役办理了身份卡片和臂章。然而，南京城陷后，日军当局并没有给予美国大使馆必要的保护。日军士兵的肆意侵入及明目张胆地抢劫，使大使馆及外交官员的财产遭受不同程度的损失。有鉴于此，美国驻上海总领事高斯请示了美国国务院之后，要阿利森在上海静候局势明朗后，再做打算。

临危受命

New York Times.

THE WEATHER
Occasional rain, with moderate temperature today. Tomorrow rain, followed by colder.

YORK, FRIDAY, DECEMBER 17, 1937. TWO CENTS

PANAY ATTACK DELIBERATE, YARNELL REPORT INDICATES; OUR PROTESTS BROADENED

Japanese Army in Three Drives On a Chinese Line of 300,000 Men

New Defense Front Is Great Semicircle From North Bank of Yangtze to Hangchow Bay —Nanking Is a Terrible Scene

By HALLETT ABEND

Wireless to The New York Times.

SHANGHAI, Friday, Dec. 17.—Even before the celebrations attendant upon the formal Japanese entry into Nanking today, the Japanese Army launched three new drives against a great semi-circle of Chinese forces estimated at thirty divisions, or more than 300,000 men, disposed on a new front with a total length of about 220 miles.

The new Chinese line ran from the vicinity of Yangchow, on the north bank of the Yangtze River across from the Kiangyin forts, to the vicinity of Hsuchow, on Tientsin-Pukow Railway northwest of Nanking, thence southward near Wuwei and across the Yangtze near Tungling. Thence the front joined the longer established Chinese lines in Chekiang Province (extending to Hangchow Bay).

The Japanese claimed they had already captured Pucheng and Wuyi, northward of Pukow along the railway, and they said another column that crossed the Yangtze near Chinkiang, about forty miles east of Nanking, had already captured Taihsin and was nearing Hwaiying, while a column that crossed near Hohsien was threatening the Chinese line in Anhwei Province.

The capitulation of Nanking has already had a profound effect on the morale of the war-weary Chinese troops in North China fronts. One force of 8,000 surrendered in Western Shantung Province, and other forces in Shangtung and Southern Hopeh, totaling 9,000, gave up their arms.

The Japanese headquarters in Nanking announced yesterday that the Japanese had taken more than 15,000 prisoners inside Nanking's walls. It was believed another 25,000 were still within the city, having discarded their uniforms, hidden their arms and donned civilian clothing.

Japanese Army and Navy spokesmen both denied yesterday any knowledge of reported pending Japanese operations in Kwangtung Province and elsewhere in South China. Informed that an increase in Japanese aerial activity in the

Continued on Page Five

GUNS RAKED VESSEL

Word That Surface Craft Fired in Clear Weather Forwarded to Tokyo

HULL, FIRM, AVOIDS HASTE

Seeks Clue as to Whether High Command or Officers on Scene Were to Blame

Official reports from Admiral Yarnell to Washington yesterday represented the sinking of the gunboat Panay and other American vessels as a deliberate act by the Japanese. No new move will be made, however, until further reports and the expected Japanese note are received. [Page 1.]

Britain also awaited a response from Tokyo to her protest, but it was said much more must be done before she would be satisfied. There was no belief that difficulties with Japan were at an end. The idea of reinforcements for Hongkong or Singapore seemed to have been dropped, although an attack on Canton was expected. [Page 4.]

Naval authorities in Tokyo announced an unprecedented mark of honor would be shown to the American dead by the firing of a salute on the shore near the place where the vessels were sunk. A reply will be sent to the United States note in a few days.

Japanese troops, following the occupation of Nanking, have spread out on the north bank of the Yangtze River. A triumphal entry is to be made into the former Chinese capital by Japanese commanders. [Page 1.]

Yarnell Tells of Attack

Special to The New York Times.

WASHINGTON, Dec. 16.—Official reports received by Secretary of State Cordell Hull concerning the Japanese attack on the United States gunboat Panay and the three

TELEGRAPH WIRES, STORES, SHIP LINE, HIT BY STRIKE WAVE

450 Tourists Left on Pier as Monarch of Bermuda Sails With Skeleton Crew

POSTAL WIRES AFFECTED

3 Woolworth Stores and 4 Taxi Fleets Are Involved in the Walkouts

A wave of strikes broke over the city yesterday, hitting transportation by land and sea, communication facilities, restaurants and department stores.

About 450 persons who had booked accommodations on the Furness Bermuda liner Monarch of Bermuda for a cruise to Nassau and Bermuda were left behind with their baggage on Pier 95, North River, when a strike of 300 members of the ship's crew forced the vessel to sail without them.

For several hours, service of the Postal Telegraph and Cable Corporation in New York and also in six other cities was interrupted when employes of the corporation held "stand-up" demonstrations in its offices.

Drivers employed by four taxicab fleets went on strike and the Transport Workers Union charged that members of the Police Department were consorting with strike-breaking "thugs."

Andrews Takes a Hand

Workers in three stores of the F. W. Woolworth Company went on strike. State Industrial Commissioner Elmer F. Andrews set up a committee to sift all aspects of their dispute and to consider the advisability of issuing a minimum wage order to stabilize the chain-store business.

Thirteen Automat pickets arrested in disturbances Wednesday evening were sentenced to two days in jail. Decisions in the cases of thirty-seven others will be given today.

CONGRESSMEN SHUN 'COALITION MOVE

Democrats Balk at Appearing to Be Rebels and Republicans Cling to Party Goal

SPONSORS STILL HOPEFUL

Bailey, Denying 'Bloc' Aim, Urges Roosevelt Assent—Vandenberg Awaits Public

SOVIET TAKES STEPS TO HOLD 'ROBINSONS'

Izvestia Intimates Mysterious Couple Already May Be Held by Moscow Authorities

PASSPORTS ARE TRACED

Investigating Officials Here Also Learn Two Sailed From New York on the Rex

Sovereigns Cool Crash in London

ALCATRAZ 'BROKEN' TWO CONVICTS

STOCKADE IN FOG

1937 年 12 月 17 日《纽约时报》关于“帕奈”号事件的报道：“帕奈”号遭到蓄意攻击

1937年8月，日本海军上将长谷川清发布公告。长谷川宣布封锁从长江口到潮州的中国海岸，并宣称在日本军舰所控制的范围内可以扣留外国的船只，以鉴别国旗和检查货物，对于船上所载被日本认为是走私的货物，日本即可扣留并享有优先购买权。9月，封锁范围有所扩大。这一行为引起了英美国家的不满。

12月1日，日本大本营发布“中国方面舰队应与陆军协力攻略南京”的大海令，并调整了华中方面海军作战序列，以一直负责长江“警备”的第11战队为核心，组建第1警戒部队负责吴淞上游长江江段作战，任命原第3水雷战队司令官近藤英次郎为第11战队司令官，并负责指挥警戒部队，开始“溯江作战”。时任日本海军炮舰“势多”号舰长的寺崎隆治回忆道：“接近南京时长江被一分为二，沿着北岸前进时不断受到两岸中国兵的攻击。这时候开始，有中国兵乘平底帆船和木筏顺流而下，并且越来越多。“势多”上有4门25毫米机关枪，于是就用机关枪边射击边前进。（中国兵）最初是向对岸浦口逃离的，但很快浦口也有日军出现，就只能向长江上游或下游逃了。随着南京的接近，不止有平底帆船和筏子，也有抱着木板、门板的中国兵，长江中满是那样的中国兵，好像完全没有考虑到日本舰队正从下游溯江而来。（利用平底帆船、筏子等逃离的中国兵）大概有数千人。‘势多’边前进边射击，后面的军舰也相继射击，总计大概 20 艘，时机可谓是正好。13 日下午 3 点 50（到达南京）。……接近下关栈桥，从望远镜中可以看到有很多（大概五百人）中国兵在挥手。中国兵大概没想到日本军舰这么早就来到，以为是中国军舰才挥手的吧。接近的同时又用 25 毫米机关枪扫射。”

当时任海军从军绘画通信员、乘坐“坶”舰前往南京的住谷磐根回忆：“接近南京时，……可以看到乘船

难民坐船逃离南京

的中国兵向浦口方向逃。于是‘坶’开炮射击，不久就看到抱着木板之类的中国兵漂流过来，到处都是。这时换用步枪射击，因为甲板离水面只有四五米，所以能百发百中……其中也有看到此景而求饶的士兵。”

对于这些日本海军的少壮派军官，阿利森并不陌生。他们中的许多人，要么是阿利森在日本海军机关学校时期曾经的同僚，要么是阿利森曾经的学生。对于日本海军的一举一动，身处上海的阿利森一直密切地关注着。

虽然日本海军舰队在部队规模及活动范围上，远逊于在南京城内外各处活动的10余万日本陆军，但由于海军是技术性兵种，舰艇火力强于陆军，且恰逢中国败兵、难民集中于江岸及江面，试图逃离南京，因此死于其暴行的中国败兵、难民人数也应有相当数量。日本《读卖新闻》12月14日报道：“我舰队XX艘，冒着敌水雷的危险，压制江岸各地敌炮台，于今日（13日）傍晚五时溯航至南京，在下关码头附近停泊，将敌密集部队陷于炮火洗礼中。”

1937年12月12日，日军攻占南京前夕，日本海军航空队所属军机对停泊在南京长江江面上的美国军舰“帕奈”号、英国军舰“瓢虫”号以及美英商船，进行了蓄意攻击，造成严重外交事件，是为美日“帕奈”号

o York Times.

THE WEATHER

Occasional rain, with moderate temperature today. Tomorrow rain, followed by colder.

YORK, FRIDAY, DECEMBER 17, 1937.

TWO CENTS

PANAY ATTACK DELIBERATE, YARNELL REPORT INDICATES; OUR PROTESTS BROADENED

Japanese Army in Three Drives On a Chinese Line of 300,000 Men

New Defense Front Is Great Semicircle From North Bank of Yangtze to Hangchow Bay —Nanking Is a Terrible Scene

By HALLETT ABEND

Wireless to The New York Times.

SHANGHAI, Friday, Dec. 17.—Even before the celebrations attendant upon the formal Japanese entry into Nanking today, the Japanese Army launched three new drives against a great semi-circle of Chinese forces estimated at thirty divisions, or more than 300,000 men, disposed on a new front with a total length of about 220 miles.

The new Chinese line ran from the vicinity of Yangchow, on the north bank of the Yangtze River across from the Kiangyin forts, to the vicinity of Hsuchow, on Tientsin-Pukow Railway northwest of Nanking, thence southward near Wuwei and across the Yangtze near Tungling. Thence the front joined the longer established Chinese lines in Chekiang Province (extending to Hangchow Bay).

The Japanese claimed they had already captured Pucheng and Wuyi, northward of Pukow along the railway, and they said another column that crossed the Yangtze near Chinkiang, about forty miles east of Nanking, had already captured Taihsin and was nearing Hwaiying, while a column that crossed near Hohsien was threatening the Chinese line in Anhwei Province.

The capitulation of Nanking has already had a profound effect on the morale of the war-weary Chinese troops in North China fronts. One force of 3,000 surrendered in Western Shantung Province, and other forces in Shantung and Southern Hopeh, totaling 9,000, gave up their arms.

The Japanese headquarters in Nanking announced yesterday that the Japanese had taken more than 15,000 prisoners inside Nanking's walls. It was believed another 25,000 were still within the city, having discarded their uniforms, hidden their arms and donned civilian clothing.

Japanese Army and Navy spokesmen both denied yesterday any knowledge of reported pending Japanese operations in Kwangtung Province and elsewhere in South China. Informed that an increase in Japanese aerial activity in the

Continued on Page Five

GUNS RAKED VESSEL

Word That Surface Craft Fired in Clear Weather Forwarded to Tokyo

HULL, FIRM, AVOIDS HASTE

Seeks Clue as to Whether High Command or Officers on Scene Were to Blame

Official reports from Admiral Yarnell to Washington yesterday represented the sinking of the gunboat Panay and other American vessels as a deliberate act by the Japanese. No new move will be made, however, until further reports and the expected Japanese note are received. (Page 1.)

Britain also awaited a response from Tokyo to her protest, but it was said much more must be done before she would be satisfied. There was no belief that difficulties with Japan were at an end. The idea of reinforcements for Hongkong or Singapore seemed to have been dropped, although an attack on Canton was expected. (Page 4.)

Naval authorities in Tokyo announced an unprecedented mark of honor would be shown to the American dead by the firing of a salute on the shore near the place where the vessels were sunk. A reply will be sent to the United States note in a few days.

Japanese troops, following the occupation of Nanking, have spread out on the north bank of the Yangtze River. A triumphal entry is to be made into the former Chinese capital by Japanese commanders. (Page 1.)

Yarnell Tells of Attack

Special to The New York Times.

WASHINGTON, Dec. 16.—Official reports received by Secretary of State Cordell Hull concerning the Japanese attack on the United States gunboat Panay and the three

TELEGRAPH WIRES, STORES, SHIP LINE, HIT BY STRIKE WAVE

450 Tourists Left on Pier as Monarch of Bermuda Sails With Skeleton Crew

POSTAL WIRES AFFECTED

3 Woolworth Stores and 4 Taxi Fleets Are Involved in the Walkouts

A wave of strikes broke over the city yesterday, hitting transportation by land and sea, communication facilities, restaurants and department stores.

About 450 persons who had booked accommodations on the Furness Bermuda liner Monarch of Bermuda for a cruise to Nassau and Bermuda were left behind with their baggage on Pier 95, North River, when a strike of 200 members of the ship's crew forced the vessel to sail without them.

For several hours, service of the Postal Telegraph and Cable Corporation in New York and also in six other cities, was interrupted when employes of the corporation held "stand-up" demonstrations in its offices.

Drivers employed by four taxicab fleets went on strike and the Transport Workers Union charged that members of the Police Department were consorting with strike-breaking "thugs."

Andrews Takes a Hand

Workers in three stores of the F. W. Woolworth Company went on strike. State Industrial Commissioner Elmer F. Andrews set up a committee to sift all aspects of their dispute and to consider the advisability of issuing a minimum wage order to stabilize the chain-store business.

Thirteen Automat pickets arrested in disturbances Wednesday evening were sentenced to two days in jail. Decisions in the cases of thirty-seven others will be given today. Meanwhile, the Horn & Hardart Company, operators of the Automat chain, announced that $230,000 in Christmas bonuses would be distributed today to 4,000 employes.

The Monarch of Bermuda, scheduled to sail at 3 P. M., was forty minutes late in pulling away from her pier.

Two hours before 200 members of the crew responded to a strike call issued by Harry Griffiths, president of the Marine Transport Union, by walking off the ship. After conferences among officials of the line it was found that a skeleton crew of

CONGRESSMEN SHUN 'COALITION MOVE'

Democrats Balk at Appearing to Be Rebels and Republicans Cling to Party Goal

SPONSORS STILL HOPEFUL

Bailey, Denying 'Bloc' Aim, Urges Roosevelt Assent—Vandenberg Awaits Public

SOVIET TAKES STEPS TO HOLD 'ROBINSONS'

Izvestia Intimates Mysterious Couple Already May Be Held by Moscow Authorities

PASSPORTS ARE TRACED

Investigating Officials Here Also Learn Two Sailed From New York on the Rex

Sovereigns Cool Crash in London

AZ 'BROKEN' O CONVICTS

STOCKADE IN FOG

1937 年 12 月 17 日《纽约时报》关于“帕奈”号事件的报道：“帕奈”号遭到蓄意攻击

事件、英日“瓢虫”号事件。“帕奈”号事件爆发之时，阿利森正在上海待命，这一严重的流血事件也为阿利森后来的第二次南京之旅平添了一份凶险。

19世纪60年代，美国根据中美《天津条约》，取得了派军舰在中国江海巡弋护商护侨的权力。1900年义和团运动之后，美国在中国长江和珠江分别设立了分舰队，以巡逻两大流域及中国沿海。1927年，美国海军长江分舰队有江河炮舰7艘，最远可上行至重庆。随后，又在上海江南造船所新建了6艘适合江河航行的炮舰，以取代已陈旧的军舰，“帕奈”号是其中1艘。“帕奈”号舰长58.3米，宽8.5米，吃水1.7米，排水量475吨，主机功率2384马力，航速15节，编制官兵65名，装有76毫米舰炮2门和7.62毫米机枪数挺。

1937年8月13日淞沪会战开始后，“帕奈”号正在长江中下游担负巡航任务。9月27日，美国海军亚洲舰队司令官哈瑞·雅内尔海军上将向驻华各舰下达命令：“在美国公民未全部离华前，我们的舰队不能撤离。”

11月下旬，日军从上海向南京迅速推进，南京形势十分危险。美国驻华使馆大部分人员和美侨乘船撤离南京。“帕奈”号舰长詹姆斯·休斯海军少校接到命令后，从汉口下行南京，执行撤运剩余的使馆人员和美侨任务。

“帕奈”号沉没时的情景

此时，舰上有官兵59人。12月9日晚，已上舰的有4名使馆工作人员、5名美国记者、2名美国商人、1名英国记者、2名意大利记者及意大利驻华副领事。11日，“帕奈”号在通知日本方面之后起航，离开南京驶向上游。不久，美孚石油公司的3艘油轮“美安”“美夏”“美平”号也驶来同行。4艘舰船都悬挂美国国旗，还在甲板上覆盖大号国旗，十分醒目。下午2时许，日本陆军第13重炮兵联队向江中行驶的4艘美国舰船开炮，所幸无一中弹。当晚，4艘美国舰船在南京上游12海里处江中抛锚。

12日上午8时14分，日军再次炮击。休斯下令各舰船继续上行。9时45分，1艘日军武装船驶近“帕奈”号，发出信号要求停航。日军大尉村上带着2名士兵登舰盘查。9时54分，在日军官兵离舰后，美国舰船继续航行。11时，舰船行至和县境内抛锚休息。此处距南京28海里。午餐后，舰船上的许多人员在打牌，记者们在抓紧工作。下午1时27分，“帕奈”号的瞭望哨突然报告说发现3架双发动机飞机从南边飞来，高度为2000多米。美国大使馆陆军副武官费兰克·罗伯特上尉举起望远镜仔细辨认后确认是日军飞机。这正是属于日本海军第13航空队的九六式舰上攻击机，是从常州机场起飞的，其领队是分队长村田重治海军航空大尉。1时38分，机群飞临“帕奈”号上，在没有任何警告的情况下，炸弹就纷纷落下。1枚炸弹击中舰艏，前主炮被炸毁，舰桥受损，无线电室被毁，锅炉舱损坏，主机瘫痪。休斯被掉下的操舵轮击中右脚，造成骨折。休斯被人救出后，副舰长阿瑟·安德斯海军上尉接替指挥，命令舰员用机枪还击。不久，安德斯被弹片击中喉咙，无法说话，但他仍用笔在纸上写命令指挥作战。福克斯电影公司的埃里克·梅尔冒着弹雨，用摄影机拍下了日机轰炸美舰的镜头。第一波日机飞去后，随后又有6架日本海军九六式舰上轰炸机、

9 架九五式舰上战斗机、6 架九四式舰上轰炸机依次前来袭击“帕奈”号，美国军舰上有限的机枪防空火力无法阻拦日机。舰体受创严重。2 时 5 分，在舱室大量进水，主甲板已被淹的情况下，安德斯下令弃舰，舰员分乘 2 艘小艇分批撤离。有的人则借助拆下的木栅、桌面泅水逃生。此间，日机向小艇和舰员登岸的芦苇丛用机枪扫射。3 时 54 分，“帕奈”号沉入江中。这是美国在第二次世界大战前被击沉的第一艘军舰。美舰官兵有 13 人重伤、32 人轻伤（含 3 名中国厨师），2 名美国大使馆工作人员和 1 名美国商人轻伤，1 名意大利记者重伤。这名意大利记者和 1 名美国士兵于次日死亡。15 日，“帕奈”号幸存者分乘美、英军舰前往上海。17 日，1 名送至上海的美国人因伤重在上海的医院去世。与“帕奈”号同行的 3 艘美国油轮也遭到轮番攻击，“美安”号船长卡尔森遇难。还有 30 名美籍船员伤亡。3 船靠岸搁浅后，人员上岸躲避。事后，美国政府向日本方面提出严重抗议，美国民众也表达了强烈愤慨，要求政府严惩日本。日本政府一方面极力辩解，一方面表示“歉意”。日本海军将指挥空袭行动的第 2 联合航空队司令官三竝贞三海军航空大佐“撤职”，长谷川清、村田重治等有关将领也受到“警告”。日本还发动几十名女学生分别写信给美国海军部“道歉”。由于美国当时不想同日本开战，在收到日本支付的221万多美元的“赔偿”后，不再追究日本的责任。

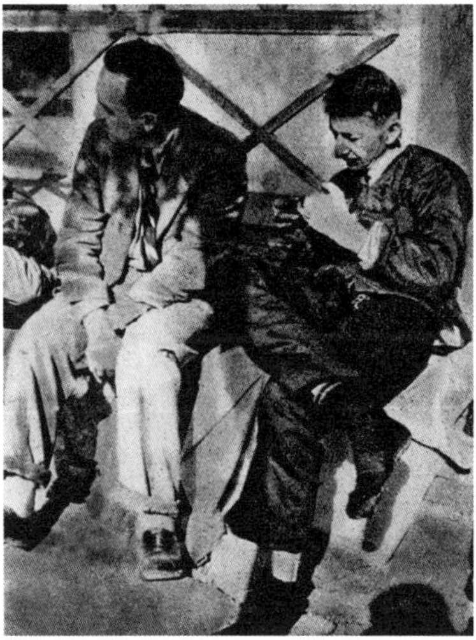

受伤的“帕奈”号舰长与美国环球公司记者谈话

此时，留在南京的美国民间人士和美国政府在如何保护美国权益问题上，存在明显分歧。民间人士认为：日本在南京和中国的暴行以及侵犯各国在华利益的行为，如果得不到及时制止，将来就可能对西方形成直接威胁。但美国官方却仍曲意争取日本的善意对待。30年代中期，德、意、日法西斯在欧洲和亚洲形成两个战争策源地。然而，此时的美国盛行孤立主义。1935年，美国国会通过旨在使美国保持中立的《皮特曼中立的决议案》。该决议案规定：战争时期禁止美国输出武器装备和信贷，而有效期为两年的“现购自运”条款则授权总统要求在美国购买非军事物资的交战国付现金并用本国船只装运。面对法西斯国家的侵略扩张，孤立主义和中立法无异于对侵略扩张的默许和纵容。

因此，日本方面认为，只要不将美日关系挑衅到直接敌对的境地，美国国内由于孤立主义势力盛行，最终都会被迫决定日本无罪。应该说，日军对国际局势的误判，也是造成日军暴戾行动的重要因素。南京沦陷后，日军对第三国在宁资产的劫掠暴行，连同日军占领南京前夕蓄意制造的美日“帕奈”号事件，可以说是日军对西方在华势力的一次重大挑战。

西方人士常驻南京，存在于南京大街小巷之中的大量西方房产由他们管理。这些人和物构成了实实在在的西方在宁利益。南京大屠杀期间，西方人士是日军南京暴行的亲历者，相对于中国难民，他们有着一定程度的自由和活动空间，他们目睹并且用不同方式记录下了日军在南京惨无人道的罪行。西方人士管理下的房产为难民提供了并非绝对安全却又无可替代的避难所。

12月13日，日军占领南京。日方通知美国外交部门，“18名留在南京的美国人都很好”“大使馆建筑没有受损”。然而，美国政府从其他渠道得到的消息，却证实日军占领下的南京正发生大规模的恐怖暴行。15、16日，

5位美英战地记者和摄影师离开南京，他们在欧美及中国报纸上发表了第一波日军暴行的报道。随后，不时有日军暴行的消息突破封锁传播出去。25日，美驻华大使詹森在发给国务卿的电报中称，日军在南京“有计划、有组织地抢劫了住所和商店”，对中国人“进行了大规模的抢劫和许多不分青红皂白的射杀和杀戮”。美国教会学校和大使馆的财物也遭到劫掠。为了有效地保护在中国的财产，美国国务院决定尽早将外交官派回南京。在这种情况下，阿利森临危受命。

阿利森时年33岁，此前在日本东京，中国大连、济南等地的美国使领馆工作的经验和出色的日语能力是他被派往南京的重要原因。除了保护美国财产之外，阿利森等外交官此行还负有重大的外交情报使命。当时，国务卿赫尔和总统罗斯福作为决策者，对日军在南京的暴行有原则上和立场上的宣示。因此，美国驻华大使詹森、驻日大使格鲁、美国驻上海总领事高斯都迫切希望了解南京形势。另有美国驻日本大使馆武官卡伯特·科维尔和美国海军亚洲舰队司令哈利·雅奈尔等，也对南京形势十分关注。

美国海军长江巡逻炮艇“瓦胡”号于1937年12月28日从上海启程。“瓦胡”号此行有三个主要任务：一、将美国外交官送往南京，重开美国驻南京大使馆；二、驶往南京上游的安徽和县水域，设法从 12 月 12 日被日军炸沉的美国炮艇“帕奈”号的残骸里打捞出重要的文件及其他物品；三、将医药用品送往美国教会开办的芜湖总医院。

阿利森搭乘“瓦胡”号于 1937 年 12 月 28 日从上海启程，12 月 31 日下午驶抵南京水域，江边一带景象惨败，枪声入耳。停泊在附近的英国炮艇“蜜蜂”号的船长哈罗德·汤姆斯·阿姆斯特朗告诉包括阿利森在内的美国官员：“仍不许外国人上岸，根据日军司令代表的说法，1 月 5 日之前都不允许上岸，理由是‘清剿残敌’的行动仍在进行之中，还不安全。”于是第二天早晨，“瓦胡”号驶往“帕奈”号沉没水域进行打捞作业。外交官协助打捞南京大使馆的财物及密码本等重要文件。

1938 年 1 月 4 日，打捞作业完毕之后，美国外交官仍没有获准在南京登岸。1 月 5 日，“瓦胡”号溯江而上驶往芜湖，将医药用品送达芜湖总医院。与此同时，阿利森等外交官查访了留在当地的美国传教士的情况，以及日军占领芜湖后美国财产受损失的程度。留在芜湖的美国传教士对阿利森等外交官说：“日军占领最初的一个星期里，‘残酷对待并屠杀平民，肆无忌惮地掳掠破坏'城内的私人财产。外国人的人身能受到尊重，但无人看管的财产一般均遭偷盗。"

几经周折后，美国领事小组最终于1938年1月6日上午11点抵达南京下关，他们是日军占领南京后首批获准进入南京城的外国官员。与阿利森同时登岸的还有副领事詹姆斯·埃斯皮（James Espy）、工作人员麦克法恩（A. A. McFadyen）等人。

詹姆斯·埃斯皮（1908—1976）出生在俄亥俄州的辛辛那提市，父亲是当地富有的银行家。1930年从耶鲁大学毕业后，他曾在剑桥大学和辛辛那提大学深造。此后曾在家乡辛辛那提的银行中工作过一段时间。1935年10月进入外交界，在美国驻墨西哥城大使馆任副领事。1937年4月调往驻上海总领事馆，同年底随阿利森前往南京。埃斯皮在南京工作勤奋，效率极高，展现了他进行调查、整理材料、撰写报告等方面的出众才华。记载日军在南京暴行最重要的两份长篇报告即由其整理撰写。

抵达南京的另一位美国外交官小阿契包德·亚历山大·麦克法恩（Archibald Alexander McFadyen. Jr., 1911—2001）出生在中国庐山牯岭一个美国传教士医生的家庭。其父阿契包德·亚历山大·麦克法恩长期在徐州行医，1938年夏曾向美国驻上海总领事馆报告日军占

小阿契包德·亚历山大·麦克法恩（Archibald Alexander Mc-Fadyen，Jr.，1911—2001）

领徐州后的残暴行径。小麦克法恩在中国长大，曾就读于上海的美国学校，以后回美国乔治亚州罗马小镇上中学，1935 年毕业于北卡罗莱纳州的大卫逊（Davidson）学院，主修经济学。大学毕业后即返回中国，供职于中华全国饥馑救济委员会。1937 年 4 月，他进入美国驻上海总领事馆任职员，同年底前往南京，参与了调查日军暴行及美国财产和权益遭破坏、损失的工作。麦克法恩和埃斯皮一起成为阿利森的得力助手。

再抵南京

1938 年初，站立在废墟前的南京难民

为应对美国使馆人员返回南京，日本占领当局做了很多粉饰太平的布置。日军开始清理街道上已经放置多时的平民百姓、妇女和儿童无辜被杀害的尸体。日军向各国使馆建筑派出了警卫，同时召集军官会议，强调严禁闯入外国使馆抢劫的行为。在码头上，美国外交官们“受到非常合作的日本领事、海军，以及军方代表的迎接”。然而，他们对日本官员的印象很快就有所改变。进入市区，历历在目的是极其凄惨的景象：整片整片的商店、建筑遭洗劫、焚烧；房屋中、池塘里或小路旁仍遗有受难者的尸骸。南京城一片凄凉。太平路、中华路和城内每条主要商业街道都成为一片废墟。城南许多主要街道也被烧毁。

留在城内的居民主要来自贫困的阶层，“绝大多数人像难民一样拥挤在‘安全区’内临时的难民营中”。老百姓在没有供水、没有电、没有邮电通讯、没有燃料供应、粮食极少的情况下谋求生存。消防队和卫生部门已不复存在。老百姓可以使用的唯一医疗设施是美国人开办的教会医院鼓楼医院。城市的公共交通系统已瘫痪，“可以看到以前在城市作为公共交通工具的公共汽车的残骸躺在路旁，要不然就是车子已被拖走，充作军用”。

在对中国老百姓施暴的同时，日军不加区别地洗劫

1938 年初，南京残破的街道

了各国驻南京的政府机构、团体组织、个人的房产。不管是外国使领馆的建筑、教会的教堂、学校的校园，还是商业机构、外国公民的私人寓所，均不同程度地遭到侵犯与破坏。1 月 6 日，阿利森刚抵南京就电文报告了日本兵造成相当多的美国财产损失和破坏，美国使馆大院里的数辆汽车也被劫走。

此时的美国使馆只有阿利森等 3 名外交人员，根本无力照看遍布南京的美国利益。阿利森得到美国权益被侵害的报告主要来自南京的美国侨民。当时留在南京的 14 名美国公民与其他西方人士一道成立国际安全区，组建难民营，开办赈济难民的粥厂，为 20 多万难民提供住房，筹措煤炭、米面，供应粮食。这些西方人士不畏艰险，义无反顾地保护、救济难民。与此同时，也设法保护在城内的美国财产与权益。然而，面对日本兵的机枪、刺刀，他们的努力显得微不足道。他们向日本当局一而再再而三地提出抗议，却无济于事。对于滞留南京的西方人士，

破败的下关、中华路、太平路

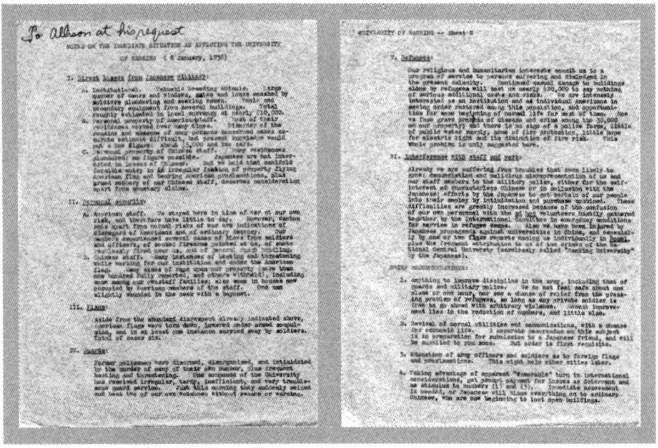

1938 年 1 月 8 日，国际安全区委员会致阿利森信函，报告金陵大学的损失以及接收难民状况

日军很不欢迎。为避免南京大屠杀的消息外泄，日军在占领南京后，封锁了水陆交通，南京成为“陆上孤岛”，这些西方人士的行动受到了严格的限制。阿利森等外交官员回到南京，使得南京的外籍人士又恢复了与外界的联系。鼓楼医院的医生威尔逊在日记中写道：“1 月 6 日，星期四。更忙碌的三天过去了，局势有了一些新的变化，日本军队渐趋平静，没什么可讲的。上午有三位美国外交人员返回。阿利森先生以前在济南，我们住进卜凯家后他曾来做过客，现在是美国驻南京领事。他带了两位年轻人。我们留他们在这儿吃了午饭，今晚他们还要赴

日本使馆做客。他们带来了一些信件，大部分是从牯岭来的家信。想要正常收到美国的来信可能还需要好长一段时间。”

米尔斯在给妻子的信件中也谈到了美国外交官的归来所带来的积极变化：

> 大使馆成员回来让我们大大地松了一口气。我们在这里很孤单，可以说，没有政府代言或庇护，任何事情都可能导致严重后果。我们不得不每天和日本兵打交道，经常一天好几次。没有其他办法，我们勉为其难。想象一下，我代表群体给日本大使馆写一封关于日本士兵骚扰美国大使馆的抗议信。在我的中国之行中，我从来没有想过自己会担当这样的重任。
>
> 派到这里的使馆成员都是新人。阿利森现在是这里的主管，他以前在南京呆过一段时间，在 12 月撤离时还不是本地职员，所以他也算这里的新成员。

美国外交官到达南京之后就立即开展工作，他们召集留在南京城的传教士、教授、医生、护士和其他人员，和他们会谈，了解情况。这些美国公民向阿利森和其他

（左起）阿利森、米尔斯、贝德士

外交官详细讲述了南京城陷与此后日军的暴行。外交官们也亲自到城市各处巡视，注意观察，进行调查，并及时向上级主管部门汇报。抵达南京当天下午5点，阿利森拍电报给在汉口的詹森大使，对南京的情况做初步而简短的汇报：

城内美国人均安然无恙。虽然最近情况有所改善，但是日军劫掠美国人财产的现象仍相当严重。房屋只受到轻微的破坏，而屋内无人看管的东西一般均被洗劫而去。和我共进午餐的几位美国人讲述了触目惊心地肆意屠杀中国平民、强奸妇女的情况，有的就发生在美国人的房产上。美孚石油公司和德士古公司的设施被闯入，库存货物遭抢，只是被抢走的数量尚不得而知。

城里总的情况正慢慢恢复正常。大使馆里有水，但没有电。食品供应较为紧缺。日军部队仍没有很好地受到约束，但相信最糟糕的状况已经结束。

美国基督教会的财物大部分分布在南京太平路与户部街。1937年12月，日军在进攻南京时，位于南京太平路的房屋被进攻日军的两发炮弹击中，房子一部分被毁。另外两处房产位于南京户部街41号圣公会大院内安德鲁·T.罗耶夫妇的住宅也被进攻的日军炮弹击中。

唯一一位与大使馆相关的遇难中国人是詹金斯的随

被日本人完全烧毁的主要商业街太平路

从，他是在保卫詹金斯住宅的过程中被抢劫者所杀害。阿利森向美国外交部建议向日方索赔，外交部索赔五千元，日方不得不同意交付给阿利森一张两千五百元的支票。阿利森替死者遗孀（在山东某地）保管支票。在美国外交部的指示下，他从日本总领事那里接收了这张支票，并且当场发表声明说，美国政府不能保证死者遗孀将会接受这一金额作为完全赔付。

双塘难民收容所位于安全区外城西南双塘地区，是美国长老会传教团的财产，由一个学校、一个教堂和一些附近建筑物组成。所长陈罗门，收容难民约 2000 人，许多难民只是晚上来收容所住宿。该所经常被日本兵劫掠，妇女常遭强奸，仅以 1 月 6 日到 7 日 24 小时为例，

1938 年初，站立在废墟前的南京难民

1938 初，南京城外的难民

就被日本兵闯入十三次，日本兵六七次闯入拖走妇女或就在难民所内奸淫妇女。难民生活，其中约有三分之二的难民自行解决膳食，其余的难民身无分文，十分贫困，自 1938 年 1 月 5 日后，安全区国际委员会向该所提供了三袋大米，并力求每天向该所提供相应数量的大米。阿利森在报告中如实记录了这些信息。

阿利森在城内商业区观察到日军肆意焚烧的残景：“对南京中心商业区的察访显示范围广大的摧毁破坏，主要街道上几乎每一座商店、建筑都被抢劫，大部分遭焚烧。这些摧毁破坏绝大多数应该是在日军进城后发生的。”1 月 14 日，阿利森在发给美国国务卿的电文中报告：

几乎每天都收到有关日军持续侵犯美国人及其财产的报告。最近的一次发生在1月12日夜间，日本兵逾墙爬进金陵中学，在一间住满难民的教室里开了两枪后，掳走一名姑娘，再翻墙而出。1月10日下午，一名全副武装的日本兵强迫金陵神学院的门卫带他上行政楼的三楼，抢去一大堆蜡烛。1月11日下午，日本宪兵闯入金陵大学美籍教授M.S.贝茨的住宅，在未经允许、没有解释的情况下，带走一名金陵中学做日语翻译的中国人。最后两起事件用来作为我1月13日中午发21号电报所提抗议的依据。

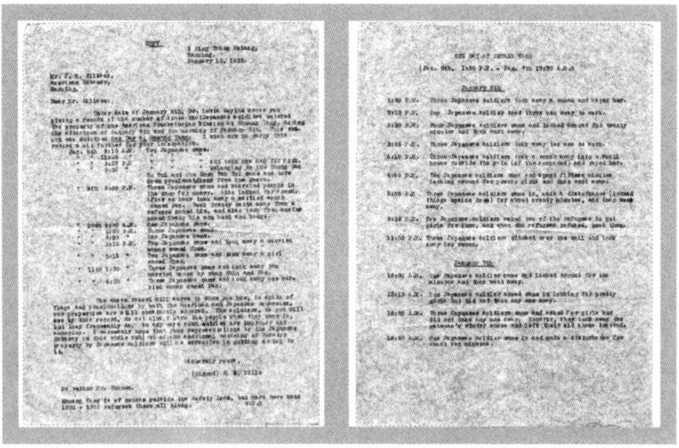

1938年1月15日，米尔斯致阿利森信函，列举日军各种暴行

1938 年 1 月 18 日，阿利森再次将 1 月 15 日以来又有 15 起日军擅闯美国人房产、洗劫财物、强奸妇女的事件报告到美国大使馆来。阿利森在 1 月 22 日所发的 32 号电报中概括描述当时南京的情况，以及美国外交官每天必须面对接踵而至的日军不法行为的报告：

> 情况虽然有所好转，军纪并未完全恢复，我仍持续收到美籍居民平均每天三次或四次在安全区内的强奸，或图谋强奸案件的报告。还有多少没有引起美国人注意的案件发生，那根本就不可能说得清。日本人现在想方设法迫使中国难民回到位于安全区外面的家里，但是，很多人不愿意回去，因为很多回去的人被抢劫、遭强奸。在数起案件中，还有人被日本兵刺死。这些事件的记录都已在本使馆存档。

除此之外，1938 年初美军情报机构所破译的日本外交电文也反映了屠杀情况。其中，日本外相广田弘毅 1 月 17 日在向日本驻美使馆发出训令时，转引英国记者田伯烈的电讯稿。该电讯稿称："自从几天前回到上海，我调查了日军在南京及周边地区所犯暴行的报告。可靠的目击者的口述记录和信誉毫无疑问的人士的信函提供

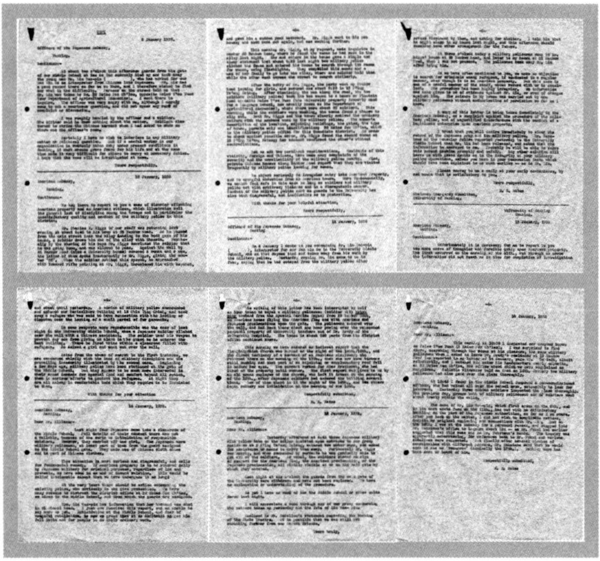

1938 年 1 月 18 日，贝德士致阿利森信函，报告日军暴行

了充分证明，即日军的所作所为及继续其暴行的手段使人联想到阿提拉及其匈奴人。至少 30 万中国平民遭到屠杀。”1938 年 1 月 21 日，詹森大使向南京美国使馆通报得自英国方面的秘密情报：“紧随日军进入南京的日本大使馆的官员们，看到日军在难民营内外公开地酗酒、杀人、强奸、抢劫，感到十分震惊。他们未能对军官们施加影响，后者漠然的态度很可能出于把放纵士兵作为对这座城市的惩罚，而且由于军队的控制，他们对致电

东京要求控制军队感到绝望，日本大使馆官员们甚至建议传教士设法在日本公布事态真相，以便利用公众舆论促使日本政府管制军队。”2月2日，阿利森等人向美

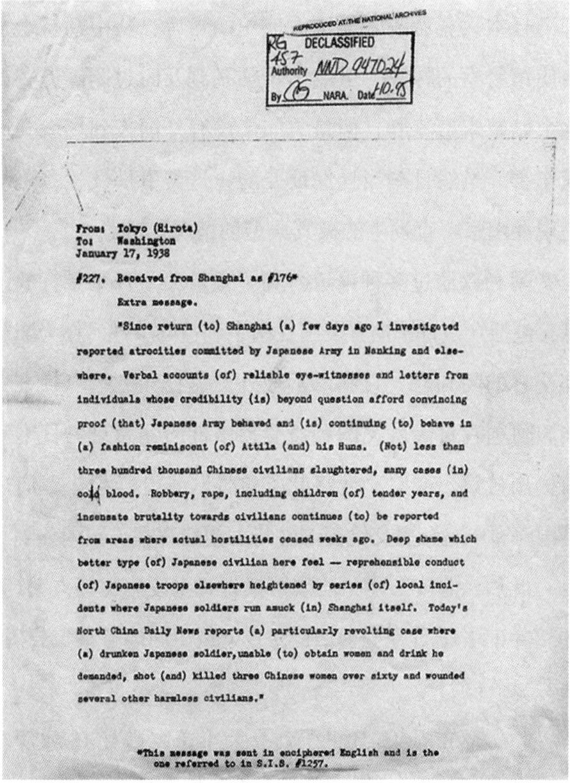

REPRODUCED AT THE NATIONAL ARCHIVES

RG 457 DECLASSIFIED
Authority NND 947024
By CS NARA. Date 10.95

From: Tokyo (Hirota)
To: Washington
January 17, 1938

#227. Received from Shanghai as #176*

Extra message.

"Since return (to) Shanghai (a) few days ago I investigated reported atrocities committed by Japanese Army in Nanking and elsewhere. Verbal accounts (of) reliable eye-witnesses and letters from individuals whose credibility (is) beyond question afford convincing proof (that) Japanese Army behaved and (is) continuing (to) behave in (a) fashion reminiscent (of) Attila (and) his Huns. (Not) less than three hundred thousand Chinese civilians slaughtered, many cases (in) cold blood. Robbery, rape, including children (of) tender years, and insensate brutality towards civilians continues (to) be reported from areas where actual hostilities ceased weeks ago. Deep shame which better type (of) Japanese civilian here feel — reprehensible conduct (of) Japanese troops elsewhere heightened by series (of) local incidents where Japanese soldiers run amuck (in) Shanghai itself. Today's North China Daily News reports (a) particularly revolting case where (a) drunken Japanese soldier, unable (to) obtain women and drink he demanded, shot (and) killed three Chinese women over sixty and wounded several other harmless civilians."

*This message was sent in enciphered English and is the one referred to in S.I.S. #1257.

广田弘毅在致日驻美国大使馆电中承认日军在南京等地用血腥手段使“不少于30万的中国平民遭杀戮”

国政府提出详细报告，说：“所有前中国士兵和那些被怀疑是的人均遭到系统杀戮。尽管得不到准确报告，但据估计，远远超过2万人被以这种方式处决。”

阿利森还记录了更多的案例。1938年1月22日晚上，三个日本兵竟然闯入美国大使馆的馆舍，从中劫持走一名使馆警察的妹妹。虽然由于阿利森及时过问、追查，这个姑娘未遭凌辱，但是“如果没有外国人到场就会造成伤害。虽然日军当局保证要防止这类事件发生，这却是现在南京一直发生的极其典型的情况”。

阿利森通过多种渠道得到了大量关于日军暴行的讯息，包括众多日军损害美国在南京利益的事件。作为职业外交官的阿利森一直都以常规外交途径和方式与日方交涉。阿利森每天就美国利益受损事件向驻南京的日本使馆提出抗议。同时，他将此类事件写入外交报告，通过美国海军电台，提交给美国驻华大使詹森和美国国务院。

此后，他接二连三地频繁报告日军侵犯美国人财产。1938年1月18日，阿利森在27号电报中向国务卿报告道：

> 从1月15日中午到今天中午，已有15件涉及日军擅自闯入美国人房产的事件报告到大使馆来。擅自闯入的过程中除了抢劫走美国公民及机构的财

产外，还强行将住在上述房屋里的10名中国妇女难民掳掠走。最近的一次，也是最声名狼藉的事件，发生在今天上午。日本兵驾驶两辆卡车闯入属于统一基督教会的大院，搬走一架钢琴和其他财物。搬钢琴时，他们毁坏了一大段院墙。该教会的一位美籍成员陈述今晨他看到院墙秋毫无损。下午1时45分围墙倒塌后我亲自去察看，并可以证明围墙是在3小时之内被毁，因为今天凌晨下雨，而地上围墙的残段完全是干的。我已多次提请日本使馆注意这些每天持续发生的事件，然而，我已被迫做出结论，要么日本大使馆无力制止这类抢劫事件，要么日军不愿或不能为美国人的财产提供适当的保护。据东京1月15日下午5时发往上海的电报，1月15日日本参谋本部曾指示南京的军事当局禁止擅闯美国产业的事件发生，但自从1月15日以来情况没有明显的好转。

阿利森的27号电报，以及其他报告日军暴行的电文引起美国最高统帅的注意。这些电报经科德尔·赫尔国务卿呈报给美国总统罗斯福。罗斯福总统阅后，于1938年1月21日向赫尔国务卿指示："请阅读所附南京的阿利森发来的 27 号电报。我觉得我们可以将这份电报或类似的电报公布出去，以此为基础来证明日本政府无力制止日本军人的这些劫掠行径，证明日军要么不愿意，要么无能为力为美国人的财产提供适当的保护。”

对于阿利森在南京提出的抗议，日本当局起初一概置之不理。对此，1938 年 4 月奉命来南京考察的另一位美国外交官考瑞尔记录道：“在南京工作的最初一段时间里，阿利森发现他向日本人提出的抗议毫无进展。总领事推诿拖延，甚至连一封简单的确认信都没有写。特务机关（tokumu kikan）也一无是处；它的联络官倒是个活泼的人，以前在渥太华当大使随员，阿利森确信，这是个很没有权威和影响力的人物，只不过是军方为达到他们自己的目的而启用的一张正面笑脸。只有当阿利森通过我们向东京交涉这些问题的时候，在南京的日本人才开始表现出对他的一些尊重或者是注意。”

有鉴于此，美国政府不得不出面直接向东京提出交涉。通过美国驻日本大使格鲁，美国政府 1938 年“1 月 17 日对日本政府发出通牒，强烈抗议日本在南京、汉口和其他地方实施军事行动过程中对美国财产的劫掠、撕毁告示、砍倒美国国旗等行为。美国政府认为日军的这些行为与日本就“帕奈”号事件通牒中的保证背道而驰，日本政府保护美国权利的措施不充分”。美国政府“要求日本政府务必强调已经发布的指示，以有效避免暴行再次发生”。针对阿利森关于日军在南京暴行的报告，美国总统罗斯福指示说：“几乎没有美国人能够反对我们保护美国人免遭一支军队的侵扰，而该军队已经不受其国内的民事政府的控制。”

面对日本当局的谎言，阿利森给予了无情的揭露和抨击。1938 年 1 月 23 日《纽约时报》报道说：“来自东京的报告显示，一项全面的命令已下达在上海和南京的军事当局，以禁止随意闯入美国人的产业。据说这是 1 月 15 日颁发的，但是阿利森先生今天报告，1 月 15 日中午到 1 月 18 日中午，美国人向他报告日军随意闯入的次数不下 15 次。”

1938 年 2 月 2 日，在南京现场的阿利森等人向美国政府提出详细报告，说：“所有前中国士兵和那些被怀疑是的人均遭到系统杀戮。尽管得不到准确报告，但据估计，远远超过 2 万人被以这种方式处决。”

围绕日本军队占据美国教会财产及限制美国人返回教会的问题，阿利森在给上级的电文中表示：“尽管在本地区对外国人行动的限制在一定程度上有所放松……但是没有迹象表明，一般的外国商人将被允许返回南京，关闭他们的现在已不再盈利的过去的生意，或是恢复他们的商业。据信除非采取特别的立场，否则等到美国或其他外国商人被允许返回时，他们将发现他们以前活动的领域在很大程度上将被日本人接管。”1938年5月上旬，随着南京周边地区驻扎日军的军事调动，许多被日军占用的教会产业被腾出，相关教会机构非常急切地希望派代表去接收这些教产。美国商人也非常担忧他们的资产，急欲前往南京探访并采取必要的措施。经过美驻华外交使领馆官员的数度交涉，至6月初，美国传教士、医生和护士始被允许返回南京，但商人依旧不被允许。在阿利森就此事问及日本外务省美国局的石井时，石井表示：“就传教士而言，只涉及美国人。如果商人被允许返回，这样就必须允许所有国家的公民返回，当局目前不希望这样做。”对此，阿利森认为：“显然，日本当局只是不想让外国商人返回南京，并将继续找借口，除非相关的政府采取更强烈的行动。”

西方侨民送出的书信、日记与报告，在国际上各种报刊刊登后，形成国际舆论，甚至对日本当局也产生了一定的压力。1938 年 1 月 22 日，斯迈思致上海“中华全国基督教总会”主席博因顿的信中写道：“从东京传来的消息说，我们发往华盛顿、柏林及伦敦的报告已经有一部分产生了效果。作为我们通过华盛顿转达抗议的结果，东京方面已经下达命令，要求在此的日军重组军队，而且据承诺，这将在三四天内完成。”果然不久，日本当局迫于国际舆论压力，改组了华中日军，召回松井石根等人。1938年4月18日，美国纽约著名的《时代》周刊发表报道称：美国的基督教和犹太慈善组织“上周在美国将南京陷落一个月之内屠杀、强奸的相当完整的目击报道和图片资料集中在一起”，进行揭露。

但是，这些信息却遭到作为当事美国“中立”政策实际执行人的国务卿科德尔·赫尔（Cordell Hull，1871—1955）的消极对待。在日本表现出侵略意图，甚至已经对中国进行大规模侵略之际，美国仍固守所谓“不干涉”政策，实际上是拒绝与其他国家采取共同行动来制止侵略战争。赫尔领导下的美国外交部门，在南京大屠杀发生之后，收到驻华外交官送交的大量有关日军南京暴行的报告，除涉及美国驻华利益问题外，美国外交部门并没有采取干预的措施，甚至没有将有关信息透露给美国舆论，客观上帮助日本掩盖了南京大屠杀暴行。

但包括罗斯福总统在内的一些美国高官却看到了打破孤立主义桎梏的契机。为了引导美国及其公众做好反法西斯战争的准备，加强美国防务力量，罗斯福与孤立主义展开了坚决而富有艺术性的斗争。1938 年 1 月，罗斯福在特别咨文中敦促立即增加 20% 的海军建设费。国会经过激烈辩论而于 5 月通过《文森扩充海军法》，准许以 10 亿美元发展海军。这一事实表明，大多数认真思考问题的美国人，已经从南京大屠杀事件中看到战争的威胁并因而同意加强防务。

“阿利森事件”

York Times.

LATE CITY EDITION

FRIDAY, JANUARY 28, 1938.

TWO CENTS

U.S. PROTESTS ANEW TO JAPAN ON MORE OUTRAGES IN CHINA; EMBASSY OFFICIAL SLAPPED

SAFEGUARDS ASKED

Note of Jan. 17 Demands Orders on Americans Be Reinforced

RELATES INSULTS TO FLAG

Official in Charge of Embassy at Nanking Hit by Soldier for Refusal to Obey Order

Demands by the United States that Japan shall take adequate measures to stop outrages on American citizens and property in China were revealed yesterday by the State Department. Britain was reported to have taken similar action. Some Washington officials took the view that attacks were deliberate, intended to drive foreigners out of China. The Tokyo Foreign Office said the strongest possible orders had been issued to the army to avoid such actions. The Cabinet decided to send an officer of high rank to deal with the situation at Nanking. [Page 1.]

John M. Allison, in charge of the American Embassy at Nanking, was slapped by a Japanese soldier when he refused to obey an order. Versions of the incident were conflicting. The Japanese apologized for the assault. [Page 12.]

Japanese planes bombed Hankow and Nanchang in reprisal raids, but failed to dampen the enthusiasm of the Chinese over their aerial success at Nanking Wednesday. Land fighting continued without materially altering the rival positions. [Page 12.]

Demands by United States

By HAROLD B. HINTON

Special to The New York Times.

WASHINGTON, Jan. 27.—Insistent demands that American lives and property be adequately safeguarded by the Japanese armies in North China have been served again upon the Foreign Office in Tokyo, the State Department announced today.

It made public, without any explanation of the delay, the text of a note presented on Jan. 17 by Jo-

'Big 3' in League Reaffirm Faith In Geneva as a Force for Peace

Eden, Delbos and Litvinoff Determined to Use It 'for All Purposes for Which It Is Fitted'—Change in Sanctions Opposed

By CLARENCE K. STREIT

Wireless to The New York Times.

GENEVA, Jan. 27.—The three great powers remaining in the League of Nations used the opening of the Council's hundredth session today to reply to the three great powers that have quit it. They answered that they have kept unshaken their faith in the League and are determined to preserve it and continue to use it "for the purposes for which it is fitted."

This note grew in force as it came successively from Anthony Eden, British Foreign Secretary; Yvon Delbos, French Foreign Minister and Maxim M. Litvinoff, Soviet Foreign Commissar. It was coupled with the assurance that the League was not and would not become an ideological bloc, except a bloc for peace.

Then after a brief statement by Foreign Minister Josef Beck of Poland, which implicitly put the League and the three signers of the Anti-Comintern Pact [Germany, Italy and Japan] on the same level and committed Poland only to cooperating with both with a view to peace, all the ten small power Council members echoed the note of the great powers. They echoed with variations reflecting their degree of faith in the great powers—and China, Sweden and Belgium clearly showed they had lost some of theirs—but all showed faith in the League and desired to see it stronger.

"His Majesty's Government in the United Kingdom," said Mr. Eden, "does not think it inappropriate at the moment, when it has to acknowledge the repudiation in some quarters of the League of Nations, to declare that its faith in the aims and ideals that inspired it remains unchanged."

He preceded this with the regretful recognition that "by the defection of some of its more important members the League is now faced with the fact that its area of cooperation is restricted, and its ability to fulfill all the functions originally contemplated for it is reduced."

Throughout he carefully avoided defining what the League could still do or could not do, leaving this as-

Continued on Page Thirteen

Housing Plan 500,000 Families

End 17 Square Miles of Bond Issue of $16,000,000 Outside Federal Program

since there is plenty of capital available for long-term investment, the Mayor said the rate could be 3 per cent or less.

As the program develops the city would increase its interest fund to perhaps one-half of 1 per cent of its total budget, the Mayor explained. His program is designed to supplement the Federal housing program, and he pointed out that the Federal program alone could not meet the entire housing problem in the city. So far as aid from the State was concerned, he said the city could not hope to receive more than $30,000,000 of the State's $50,000,000 allocation. That amount would provide new housing for about 5,000 families, a small percentage of the city's actual requirements, the Mayor's message said.

The Mayor's announcement was made public at the Board of Estimate meeting in City Hall. Mayor La Guardia was in Springfield, Ill., last night to speak on farm problems before members of the Illinois Agricultural Association. Outlining

Continued on Page Two

BURKE CALLS NLRB A 'CURSE' TO LABOR; DEMANDS INQUIRY

Board Causes Great Strife and Is Partly to Blame for Recession, He Tells Senators

SAYS IT FAVORS THE C. I. O.

He Condemns Its Hearings as Prejudiced—Other Senators Oppose Investigation

Senator Burke, testifying before a judiciary subcommittee, assailed the NLRB as a "curse" to labor and as partly to blame for the recession. [Page 1.]

Printers union refused to pay A. F. of L. assessment to fight C. I. O.; President Howard threatened I. T. U. referendum to secede if A. F. of L. council forced action. [Page 9.]

United Mine Workers ousted a Negro delegate who admitted that he was a deputy sheriff, and also voted limited autonomy for some districts. [Page 9.]

Mayor Hague announced in

VETERANS DEMAND WIDOW, ORPHAN AID

Leaders of Three of Largest Organizations Appear Before House Committee

INSIST ON FIXED PENSIONS

Proposed Bill Would Have $22 a Month Minimum, With Additions for Children

Special to The New York Times.

WASHINGTON, Jan. 27.—A drive for general pensions for widows and orphans of all World War veterans, regardless of the cause of death of the veteran, was opened today by the American Legion, the

BRIDGE AT NIAGARA PITCHES INTO GORGE

Huge Steel Structure After 24-Hour Fight Is Thrust Over by Ice Mountains

ROAR SHAKES THE CLIFFS

Thousands of Spectators Gaze With Awe as Forty-Year Scenic Span Collapses

Special to The New York Times.

NIAGARA FALLS, N. Y., Jan. 27.—A dramatic twenty-four-hour conflict of ice against steel reached a climax just after 4 o'clock this afternoon when the Falls View International Bridge collapsed into

1938 年 1 月 28 日《纽约时报》：美国再度抗议日本在华暴行　使馆外交官遭到掌掴

对于持续不断的日军暴行，以及对美国财产的侵犯，阿利森一而再再而三地提出抗议；同时，向美国国务院以及美国驻东京大使馆报告，并通过华盛顿与东京向南京的日军当局施加压力。由此，阿利森极度惹恼了南京的日军当局，使他成为在南京极不受日军欢迎的人物。日本驻南京代总领事福井淳公然指责阿利森“只听信那些偏信中国人言词的美国传教士”，他“不应该过于信任他们的抱怨”。为了反驳这一指责，阿利森决定“亲自调查下一个报告来的日军擅闯案件”。不料在调查过程中，阿利森却被日本兵打了耳光，此事最终发展成美日外交纠纷的“阿利森事件”。

日军占领南京期间，对外国人的行动和活动严加限制，不允许他们出城。阿利森到达南京两天后报告道，日军严禁人们在天黑之后出城，美国使馆的工作人员则是唯一能在白天出城的外国人。实际上，美国使馆的工作人员也只有在事先做了安排才能获准出城。美国外交官在城内实际上也不能自由行动。阿利森无论什么时候离开使馆大院，都要由一名日本宪兵陪同“保护”他。阿利森指出：“日军限制外国人来往于上海南京之间的真正原因是怕说出日本人在此所作所为的真相，而不是所宣称的关心外国人的安全。”

York Times.

LATE CITY EDITION

FRIDAY, JANUARY 28, 1938. PP TWO CENTS

U.S. PROTESTS ANEW TO JAPAN ON MORE OUTRAGES IN CHINA; EMBASSY OFFICIAL SLAPPED

Housing Plan 500,000 Families

End 17 Square Miles of Bond Issue of $16,000,000 Outside Federal Program

since there is plenty of capital available for long-term investment, the Mayor said the rate could be 3 per cent or less.

As the program develops the city would increase its interest fund to perhaps one-half of 1 per cent of its total budget, the Mayor explained. His program is designed to supplement the Federal housing program, and he pointed out that the Federal program alone could not meet the entire housing problem in the city. So far as aid from the State was concerned, he said the city could not hope to receive more than $30,000,000 of the State's $50,000,000 allocation. That amount would provide new housing for about 6,000 families, a small percentage of the city's actual requirements, the Mayor's message said.

The Mayor's announcement was made public at the Board of Estimate meeting in City Hall. Mayor La Guardia was in Springfield, Ill., last night to speak on farm problems before members of the Illinois Agricultural Association. Outlining

Continued on Page Two

'Big 3' in League Reaffirm Faith In Geneva as a Force for Peace

Eden, Delbos and Litvinoff Determined to Use It 'for All Purposes for Which It Is Fitted'—Change in Sanctions Opposed

By CLARENCE K. STREIT

Wireless to THE NEW YORK TIMES.

GENEVA, Jan. 27.—The three great powers remaining in the League of Nations used the opening of the Council's hundredth session today to reply to the three great powers that have quit it. They answered that they have kept unshaken their faith in the League and are determined to preserve it and continue to use it "for the purposes for which it is fitted."

This note grew in force as it came successively from Anthony Eden, British Foreign Secretary; Yvon Delbos, French Foreign Minister and Maxim M. Litvinoff, Soviet Foreign Commissar. It was coupled with the assurance that the League was not and would not become an ideological bloc, except a bloc for peace.

Then after a brief statement by Foreign Minister Josef Beck of Poland, which implicitly put the League and the three signers of the Anti-Comintern Pact (Germany, Italy and Japan) on the same level and committed Poland only to co-operating with both with a view to peace, all the ten small power Council members echoed the note of the great powers. They echoed with variations reflecting their degree of faith in the great powers—and China, Sweden and Belgium clearly showed they had lost some of theirs—but all showed faith in the League and desired to see it stronger.

"His Majesty's Government in the United Kingdom," said Mr. Eden, "does not think it inappropriate at the moment, when it has to acknowledge the repudiation in some quarters of the League of Nations, to declare that its faith in the aims and ideals that inspired it remains unchanged."

He preceded this with the regretful recognition that "by the defection of some of its more important members the League is now faced with the fact that its area of cooperation is restricted, and its ability to fulfill all the functions originally contemplated for it is reduced."

Throughout he carefully avoided defining what the League could still do or could not do, leaving this ex-

Continued on Page Thirteen

SAFEGUARDS ASKED

Note of Jan. 17 Demands Orders on Americans Be Reinforced

RELATES INSULTS TO FLAG

Official in Charge of Embassy at Nanking Hit by Soldier for Refusal to Obey Order

Demands by the United States that Japan shall take adequate measures to stop outrages on American citizens and property in China were revealed yesterday by the State Department. Britain was reported to have taken similar action. Some Washington officials took the view that attacks were deliberate, intended to drive foreigners out of China. The Tokyo Foreign Office said the strongest possible orders had been issued to the army to avoid such actions. The Cabinet decided to send an officer of high rank to deal with the situation at Nanking. [Page 1.]

John M. Allison, in charge of the American Embassy at Nanking, was slapped by a Japanese soldier when he refused to obey an order. Versions of the incident were conflicting. The Japanese apologized for the assault. [Page 12.]

Japanese planes bombed Hankow and Nanchang in reprisal raids, but failed to dampen the enthusiasm of the Chinese over their aerial success at Nanking Wednesday. Land fighting continued without materially altering the rival positions. [Page 12.]

Demands by United States

By HAROLD B. HINTON

Special to THE NEW YORK TIMES.

WASHINGTON, Jan. 27.—Insistent demands that American lives and property be adequately safeguarded by the Japanese armies in North China have been served again upon the Foreign Office in Tokyo, the State Department announced today.

It made public, without any explanation of the delay, the text of a note presented on Jan. 17 by Jo-

BURKE CALLS NLRB A 'CURSE' TO LABOR; DEMANDS INQUIRY

Board Causes Great Strife and Is Partly to Blame for Recession, He Tells Senators

SAYS IT FAVORS THE C. I. O.

He Condemns Its Hearings as Prejudiced—Other Senators Oppose Investigation

Senator Burke, testifying before a judiciary subcommittee, assailed the NLRB as a "curse" to labor and as partly to blame for the recession. [Page 1.]

Printers union refused to pay A. F. of L. assessment to fight C. I. O.; President Howard threatened I. T. U. referendum to secede if A. F. of L. council forced action. [Page 9.]

United Mine Workers ousted a Negro delegate who admitted that he was a deputy sheriff, and also voted limited autonomy for some districts. [Page 9.]

Mayor Hague announced in

VETERANS DEMAND WIDOW, ORPHAN AID

Leaders of Three of Largest Organizations Appear Before House Committee

INSIST ON FIXED PENSIONS

Proposed Bill Would Have $22 a Month Minimum, With Additions for Children

Special to THE NEW YORK TIMES.

WASHINGTON, Jan. 27.—A drive for general pensions for widows and orphans of all World War veterans, regardless of the cause of death of the veteran, was opened today by the American Legion, the

BRIDGE AT NIAGARA PITCHES INTO GORGE

Huge Steel Structure After 24-Hour Fight Is Thrust Over by Ice Mountains

ROAR SHAKES THE CLIFFS

Thousands of Spectators Gaze With Awe as Forty-Year Scenic Span Collapses

Special to THE NEW YORK TIMES.

NIAGARA FALLS, N. Y., Jan. 27.—A dramatic twenty-four-hour conflict of ice against steel reached a climax just after 4 o'clock this afternoon when the Falls View International Bridge collapsed into

1938 年 1 月 28 日《纽约时报》：美国再度抗议日本在华暴行 使馆外交官遭到掌掴

1938年1月25日，阿利森接到有关日军闯入金陵大学行凶的报告。1938年1月25日，金陵大学的美籍教授贝德士向阿利森报告，前一天晚上，全副武装的日本兵强行闯入美国人开办的金陵大学农具店，劫持并轮奸了一名妇女。贝德士和另一名美国教授查尔斯·亨利·里格斯（中文名林查理）仔细询问了那名妇女，向她了解情况。贝德士在这封求助信中写道：

亲爱的阿利森先生：

接着今天早晨的信，应当说，里格斯先生和我小心翼翼地带上昨天晚上胡家菜园11号劫持事件的受害妇女，我们给她一次无偏见的机会，让她回溯被劫持的路线。她非常清晰地辨认出那栋她在里面被强奸了三次的建筑。她返回的时候走错了路，那是因为在正确的路线上找不到特点明显的标志。我们总共核对了五次，看来是不会有错了。那栋建筑正是这个地区的军警办公室，就像小粉桥32号的军警办公室一样。

对这些正派民众之敌的所作所为的持续报告并没有带来什么缓解。看来已经到了必须把包括军官和士兵在内的所有人员都扫地出门的时候了。事实已经完全证明，只要他们在这里，这个地区就不会有安全。同样地，日本大使馆的人到目前为止没有采取任何可以采取的措施，因此也就无法取得任何成果。

今天下午，我接到了一个求救电话，于是就去帮忙对付闯进金银街 8 号的日军，这栋房子尽管不是我们的地产，但和我们的蚕业大楼（Sericulture Building）处于同一个栅栏区内。昨天，这些士兵穿过我们的大楼进入那栋房子实施了强奸。受害妇女在昨天夜间被送进大学避难。今天，士兵们再次前来，没有发现女人，于是愤怒地抢劫了男人们，砸碎了窗户。这个案例说明，我们美国人的福祉依赖于这个城市全局的体面风纪，而非依赖于日本当局对美国人财产的偶尔关注。这栋房屋在过去一周内被士兵们闯入了五次，并且不止一次地从我们的蚕业大楼区域内穿过。只是在今天，当居民们的处境越来越严峻时，他们才冒险向他们所知的这个区域里唯一可以提供帮助的来源求助。

在稍后的一封信件中，贝德士对此做出了更详细的描述：

亲爱的阿利森先生：

在有时间更全面地报告昨天在大学里发生的事情之前，我必须把今天晚上七点一群有醒目臂章的日本士兵对我们在胡家菜园11号的农具商店进行的一次造访的情况告诉你。

他们用枪威胁店员，对他进行搜身。接着，他们带走了一位妇女并强暴了她，两个小时以后才释放了她。相信她能辨认出被带去的那个地方，我们将努力获得相关信息以及其他可了解的详细情况。

这一案件涉及强行的不法闯入、使用武器恫吓、绑架和强奸，据推测是军警所为（根据臂章判断，唯一的其他微小可能就是特务机关）。

我们这里没有秩序和安全，用公告和国旗标示的美国财产没有得到尊重，连日军的公告和命令也没有得到尊重。

谨上

附笔：写完这封信以后，我得到了确切的告知，那些士兵从门上扯下了日军的公告。

阿利森对此事极为重视，决定亲自前往调查，并就此案件照会了日本使馆，并安排和日方进行联合调查。

1 月 26 日下午，在日本使馆警察和便衣宪兵的陪同下，阿利森、里格斯、那名妇女，以及另外两名中国人，一起到案发地点去指认强奸犯。日本人允许妇女和另一名中国人进院子。此刻，阿利森和里格斯停下来就他们是否应该陪妇女进去交换了意见。

1 月 26 日，日本领事馆警备官武富与两名宪兵找到了里格斯，然后他们一起去美国使馆拜访阿利森。阿利森与他们返回金陵大学，前往那名中国妇女被劫持的校园工场调查。据受害妇女称，日本士兵曾将她带到邻近的房子里，之后又将她释放回工场。日方人员想把那位妇女带到曾用来拘禁她的房子，阿利森、里格斯及日方人员很快到达该地。“这所房屋并非美国财产，但应是第三方财产。该房已为日本军事驻扎地，但是初到时从外表无法判断。”中国妇女被带进该房后，阿利森和里格斯随后跟了进来。

英国外交官普利多 · 布龙在报告中描述：阿利森和里格斯等人“刚迈进门口一两步，一名日本卫兵突然出现。阿利森被打了一耳光，里格斯的领结被撕下。一位日本军官则走过来大声谩骂美国人。与美方人员一起的日本宪兵企图调停，但是他们也与军方人员争吵起来。宪兵刚一提到这两个外国人是美国人时，在场的军方人员立刻暴怒起来”。

提及此事的还有鼓楼医院的医生威尔逊：

> 为了维护公众权益，阿利森理所当然地设法干涉了这件事。日本人却当众殴打他，显然想抢占理由。贝德士详细记载了事件过程，非常值得一读。我将简单讲述阿利森请他报告非法闯入美国房屋的案件。据查理·里格斯说，有天夜里11点，3名日本宪兵闯入（金陵）大学农学院（与查理·里格斯的店铺有段距离），带走一位妇女到他们的总部，强奸了3次，才把她放了回来，这件事报告给阿利森。贝德士和里格斯带那位妇女一起去辨认她被掳去的地方之前，阿利森和里格斯就和几位日本领事馆警察去了那个蛮横施暴的地方，日本人狡辩宪兵在履行他的职责，这纯粹是废话。那个日本警察于是把这位妇女带到日本大使馆询问，阿利森要求日本领事福井先生保证那位妇女的人身安全。过去发生了一个类似的案件，一个中学的男孩，彻底失踪，肯定死了。答应两小时，她却被扣了30小时，他

们真是太狡猾了。昨晚10点，他们把她带到我们的房子，列举出她的故事里的5个错误。这些错误是墙的颜色、台阶的级数、灯的位置和她被强奸的时间。就事件本身来说，没有什么分歧。他们列出这些错误，是想保住他们的面子。那个妇女被放回，我想这件事就这么结束了。

而阿利森本人在报告中是这样回忆当时的场景：

因为以往中国人指控日本人做坏事受到恐吓，里格斯先生不希望妇女单独进去。宪兵说我们最好不要进屋，但并没有肯定地说我们不能进去。一名宪兵强行带走妇女，穿过敞开的院门，后面跟着里格斯先生。我跟在后面，刚刚走进大门，我俩停下来商量。正商量间，一个日本兵愤怒地冲过来，用英语大声嚷嚷：“退出去！退出去！”与此同时，把我往后推向大门。我慢慢向后退，还没来得及出门，他就打了我的耳光。然后转身同样打了里格斯先生。和我在一起的宪兵只稍微做了制止日本兵的动作，其中一个宪兵用日语说“这些是美国人”，或者意思差不多的话。这时我们已到大门外的街上。

> 一听说我们是美国人，那个日本兵气得脸色发青，重复“美国人”这个词，并企图袭击离他最近的里格斯先生。宪兵制止了他，但他已把里格斯的衬衫的衣领和纽扣撕扯下来。此时，这个部队的指挥官出现了，对我们无礼地大声叫喊。里格斯和我没有碰过日本兵，除了和跟我们在一起的宪兵说过话，我们没有和任何日本兵讲过一句话。

事后，日本军方发言人狡辩说：“这起事件缘于阿利森傲慢的态度，他对待日本士兵犹如警察对待不法之徒。这件事也必定是阿利森不顾其外交官身份，采取公开批评日军的态度所致。”阿利森本人则否认被打之前与日本卫兵有过任何语言的交流，强调决没有碰任何一名日本士兵，也决没有跟同行的警察之外的任何人说话。阿利森还指出，里格斯也被日本卫兵打了一记耳光。在犹豫一番之后，阿利森最终决定将此事件上报给美国国务院。

1938年1月28日，美国政府电令驻东京大使格鲁，要求其向日本外务省提出抗议。美国政府将“阿利森事件”与其他侵害美国利益事件联系在一起，强调“在考虑该事件的严重性时，是考虑这样的事实，即整个事件，包括美国外交人员被日本士兵打耳光并非孤立的案例，而只是其中之一，并且与日本士兵多次非法侵入美国财产和漠视美国的权益是联系在一起的”。美国政府要求得到日本外务省“适当的道歉和保证日本政府将采取充分的措施惩罚冒犯者”。

对日军来说，“阿利森事件”的真相并不难以查明。事发当晚，日军高官就已经得到了这一事件的详细报告。1938 年 1 月 26 日，上海派遣军参谋长饭沼守少将在日记中清楚地记载了日本宪兵的调查发现：1 月 24 日夜 11 时左右，日本兵去金陵大学校园工场内美国人经营的农具商店，用刺刀威胁看店人，带走两个女人强奸后，过了两个小时左右才将她们放走。“根据受害者的陈述，实施强奸的房子确认时，由于是天野中队长及十几名士兵住宿的地方，在要进屋调查时，两个美国人也想进去。天野让士兵武装集合，反过来殴打并赶走了美国人。接到通知，本乡参谋随即去了现场，想进中队长房间却很难。隔壁房间里有三四个支那女人，当强行进入了天野房间时，他像和女人睡觉的样子，有个女人从床上下来。因此询问了中队长，中队长说，他利用手中权力，不断带来女人，付给她们钱，让士兵奸淫的。”

迫于外交压力，日方不得不同意解决“阿利森事件”

纠纷，阿利森本人得到日方多次道歉，肇事日军官兵被送交军法会议，似乎说明日方的军纪是严明的。然而，其他西方人士的经历表明，事实并非如此。此前也曾发生多起日本士兵伤害西方人士的事件，西方人士将之写成报告交给日本使馆，甚至直接向日本军方递交抗议信，却没有一个日本士兵因此受到军方惩处。西方人士在“阿利森事件”之前，“从未听说违纪事件受过任何重罚”。日军伤害西方人士并非个案，但作为肇事日军士兵受到军法追究的案例，“阿利森事件”却是个案。

“阿利森事件”的后续效应还包括日本当局被迫允许身处南京的美国人士离开南京。约翰·拉贝认为日本

1938 年 2 月，国际安全区主席约翰·拉贝离开南京前，相关人员前来送行

方面批准外籍人士离开南京有些“出乎意料”，他这样写道：

> 我认为此事有点奇怪。……昨天晚上在我请求福井批准费吴生先生出入城申请的时候，还遭到了他的粗暴拒绝。今天，他们对美国人可能好说话一些，因为这几天，他们和美国人之间发生了一些不愉快的事件。昨天，一名日本士兵竟然出手击中美国大使馆代办阿利森先生的脸部，此事被立即通报了华盛顿，今天作为伦敦广播的最新消息传到了这里。

不辱使命

1938 年，安全区内的难民在接受疫苗注射

阿利森并没有因为被打事件而停止与日本占领当局的外交斗争。在南京的 8 个月中，他始终忠实地履行他的外交职责，为保护美国财产、权益和维护中国难民的人道待遇做出了不懈的努力，也给后人留下大量涉及南京大屠杀期间以及之后南京状况的珍贵记录。

1938 年 2 月 18 日，在日方的持续压迫下，南京安全区国际委员会改组为南京国际救济委员会，放弃对安全区的管理职能，专注于救济难民的事务。23 日，原国际委员会主席拉贝离开南京。随着国际委员会的改组，日本当局通过自治委员会彻底接收了原国际委员会对安全区的部分市政管理职能。在此前后，日方解散了其中大部分的难民营，要求中国难民回到原住所。但是，在原安全区范围之外，治安状况依然很差，返回家中的难民遭到日军的屠杀、强奸和抢劫。在这种情况下，以阿利森为代表的西方外交官所面临的状况无疑变得更加险恶。

1938 年 1 月，安全区库存的盐、米等生活物资即将告罄，因营养不良，难民中的脚气病例开始出现，迫切需要大量物品供应来阻止这场灾难。而日军将原本由南京市政府划拨给国际委员会的大部分粮食强行扣押，虽经多次交涉，仍然不予归还。不仅如此，日军还拒绝了国际委员会从外地购置粮食的申请。阿利森在电文中也

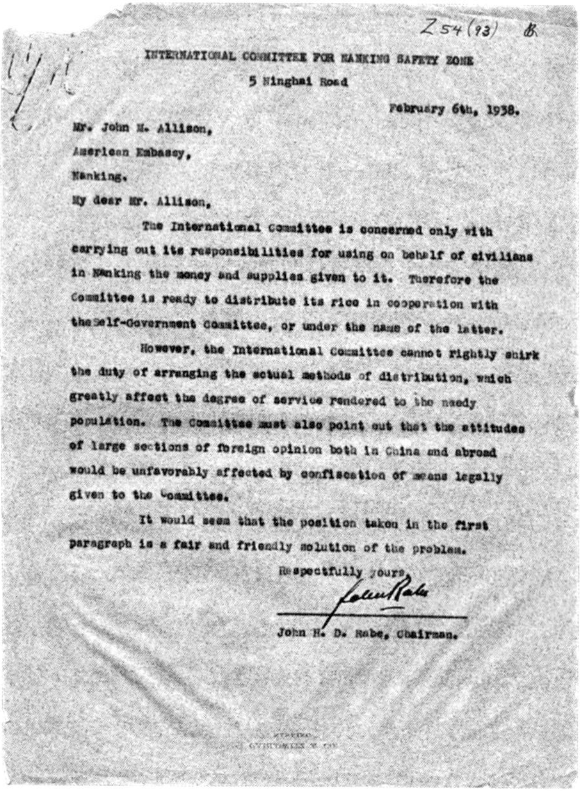

Z54 (93)

INTERNATIONAL COMMITTEE FOR NANKING SAFETY ZONE
5 Ninghai Road

February 6th, 1938.

Mr. John M. Allison,
American Embassy,
Nanking.

My dear Mr. Allison,

The International Committee is concerned only with carrying out its responsibilities for using on behalf of civilians in Nanking the money and supplies given to it. Therefore the Committee is ready to distribute its rice in cooperation with the Self-Government Committee, or under the name of the latter.

However, the International Committee cannot rightly shirk the duty of arranging the actual methods of distribution, which greatly affect the degree of service rendered to the needy population. The Committee must also point out that the attitudes of large sections of foreign opinion both in China and abroad would be unfavorably affected by confiscation of means legally given to the Committee.

It would seem that the position taken in the first paragraph is a fair and friendly solution of the problem.

Respectfully yours,

John H. D. Rabe, Chairman.

1938 年 2 月 6 日，国际安全区主席约翰·拉贝致阿利森信函，请求帮助救济难民

将日军的这些违反国际法的举动报告给美国政府。阿利森还给在南京的美国人士提供力所能及的帮助。斯迈思在日记中记录道：“阿利森和埃斯皮正帮助我们从上海

驶来的船只上获得供给。我们得到通知，……将和他们联合成立鼓楼合作供应社，还要船运一批奶粉。”拉贝在2月16日的日记中也写道：“美国大使馆的阿利森先生带来消息说，‘蚕豆问题’已获解决，已准许运进蚕豆，既可以在安全区内也可以在安全区外予以分发。”

阿利森还协助了由南京国际救济委员会组织的重建委员会的活动。到了3月份，重建委员会非常繁忙。首先是开通难民到上海的通道。重建委员会和自治委员会达成特别协议，少量难民由此获得了去上海的铁路通行许可证。

阿利森在难民银行服务问题上也提供了力所能及的协助，他几次给上海的银行写信，希望能通过美国驻华使领馆之手，替部分难民提取存折或者存款单上的资金。到3月底，获得现金救济的家庭总数达到12 145户。所发资金总数为42 725元，平均每户3.52元。在南京几乎有1/7家庭领到救济金。

除了食品和救济物资，阿利森还排除各种困难，积极推动医疗力量进入日军占领下的南京。斯迈思在书信中记录道：“美国大使馆的阿利森先生仍然在推动关于准许医生和护士进入南京的事宜。今天，日本人提议向我们提供了日本军医，但是医院方面拒绝了，尽管我们总体上会接受他们在难民营和安全区提供的帮助。阿利森先生建议，医生和护士一旦获得许可就可以坐火车前来。”

占领南京之后，日本人迫不及待地成立一个傀儡政权来控制老百姓。1938 年 1 月，日方扶持的所谓“自治委员会”成立，并在南京鼓楼举行仪式。3 月 28 日，日方扶持成立了南京维新政府。此后，日军在很多方面的行动交由这个傀儡政权出面，如掩埋尸体、街道清洁、征发夫役等等。但是，由日本大使馆集体操作建立的自治委员会和维新政府，很多时候并不能得到日本军方的认同。此时，日军的暴行继续，包括自治委员会成员都成为日军暴行的受害者，首任委员会会长陶锡三家中也被日军洗劫，陶随即提出辞职。

阿利森密切注视着全国维新政权的酝酿、成立的动向，及时报告了维新政府的领导成员、官员以及可能采取的政策。阿利森的电报报告了南京自治委员会的成立。他评论道，这些委员会的成员可以说没有一个是资深的政治人物。这个在日军特务机关监督下的委员会不仅必须得到日军特务机关的同意才能行事，而且除非在事先能肯定得到允许，它绝对不敢提出开展工作的建议。在维新政府举行就职典礼之际，不仅在举行典礼活动的中心地区布满了日军警戒部队，全城各处都有部队巡逻警戒。就职典礼前两天就禁止附近村庄的老百姓进入南京城。典礼结束后两天，维新政府的高级官员便纷纷回到上海，将这一政权的实际操作运行留给低级官员和日本人。维新政府的重要会议也都是在上海而不是在南京举行。阿利森还报告了日本人扶植的北平政权和南京维新政府之间的龃龉，以及官员相互间的勾心斗角。

阿利森还记录了日本人控制南京的金融与经济的企图。日本官员告诉美国大使馆的工作人员，如果在南京的日本商店购买东西，必须付日元。日军当局命令南京的中国官员将中国币与日元间的兑换率定在一元中国币兑七角日元上。在当地的一家银行，一名美国使馆的工作人员试图以美元兑换中国币或日元的努力都遭到拒

傀儡政权建立后组织的民众游行

绝。他被告知“在任何情况下”都不会收美元。他在中国人和日本人经营的商店里兑换美元的尝试也没有成功。这些商店告诉他，中国币只有在打20%折扣的情况下才能收。据说这是“固定的兑换率”，但却没有说明是谁定的。阿利森还注意到有大量10元、5元、1元以及50分和10分不等的日本军票在南京流通。

在日本人的统治下，贩卖毒品的现象也很严重。阿利森不仅报告自治委员会的成员本人吸食鸦片，而且指出贩卖鸦片的小商贩从日军特务机关获取鸦片。还发现在一家招待日军的饭馆里年轻女郎吸食的鸦片均是日本兵提供的。可以相信，鸦片的销售即使不是由日军倡导，日军当局也是详悉就里的。美国大使馆的工作人员在大街上亲眼见到公开出售吸食鸦片的用具。

1938年4月间，美国驻日大使馆外交官科维尔从东京出发到达中国，考察日军占领后南京、上海等地的局势。他在南京访问了美国大使馆的阿利森等人。他还在乘坐美英军舰期间，与舰上的军官及同船的商人交谈，了解他们对南京局势的讯息。科维尔将此次旅行的笔记提交给格鲁，以供美国政府对日本占领下中国长江中下游形势做出判断。科维尔在报告中谈及了阿利森的工作：

到达大使馆后，我在阿利森和埃斯皮的办公室（以前是艾奇逊的办公室）里与阿利森进行了一次炉边谈话，还会见了驻守在大使馆的美国职员和负责无线电通讯的海军官兵们。一般情况下，他们是与长江上的美国炮舰和上海进行联络；但在紧急状况下也可能直接发送到美国。这里独立于城市供电系统，电流来自于一台汽油发动机充电的电池。

金陵大学的贝德士博士和斯迈思博士来大使馆与阿利森、埃斯皮和我一起用餐。晚上，我们详细地交流了信息，他们对日本的情况也同样感兴趣。他们读了我写的关于战争开始六个月以后的日本经济的报告，我口头补充了目前为止的情况。

我听他们讲述了他们在南京的一系列经历，这是阿利森所作报告的大部分内容，大家还以个人经历进行补充，扩大了叙述范围。

阿利森还努力协调与其他西方国家外交机构的关系。英国外交部驻华官员豪尔于 1938 年 1 月 13 日在上海向英国外交部发来电报，说美国同行（阿利森）秘密告诉他，日本当局就士兵闯入美国大使馆并抢走汽车的外交事件道歉。豪尔报告说，英国大使馆内也发生了同样的事情。英国外交部认为，日本人主动向美国人道歉而不向他们道歉是其惯用伎俩，主要想在英国和美国之间打进一个“楔子”。外交部指示豪尔，可以向日本人要求道歉和赔偿，但是不能提美国，因为他们是以保密的形式提供情报的。

在与阿利森磋商之后，1月15日，豪尔又给英国外交部发来了关于南京大屠杀的最新报告：“日本高级指挥官对日本士兵的上述行为熟视无睹，这有可能是日本军队故意放纵士兵，以作为惩罚南京的手段。由于日本大使馆官员无法对日军高级将领施加影响，同时急于绕过军方的控制向东京报告上述情况，因此日本大使馆官员甚至暗示传教士，设法将这些事实在日本公之于众。这样日本政府就会在公众舆论的压力下，将会制止军队的行为。”

英国外交部官员对豪尔的电报评论道：“我相信任何日本报纸都不敢发表这些消息，由于玷污了日本皇军的荣誉，他们的办公室将会被爱国者洗劫，编辑要被谋杀。如果日本人能够庄严地向我们保证，日本水兵偷鸡事件是‘偶发事件’，那么前述行为对日本官员来说是令人难以置信的。我甚至怀疑日本民众是否会相信他们诚实、善良、勤劳的丈夫、儿子、兄弟真会干出这些事来。”

南京大屠杀过后半年多，英国外交部在上海的一位官员往伦敦发送了一封怡和洋行的代表霍伊前往南京和芜湖考察的备忘录。霍伊在备忘录中写道：“城市的受损范围达到 20% ~ 25%。太平路是最早遭到劫掠的，被日军焚烧成灰烬，毁坏程度为 90% ~ 95%。目前，很多被烧毁的中国商店的底楼被当成日军的马厩。”

到 1938 年 6 月，南京城内的安全状况已经大为改观之时，刚刚从上海回到南京的金陵大学化学系教授詹姆斯·克劳德·汤姆森坐着人力车在南京的大街上，日本哨兵拦住去路。哨兵首先检查人力车苦力的良民证，接着搜查人力车，最后讯问汤姆森博士并搜查了他。搜查的过程中，汤姆森博士没有任何反抗哨兵的行为。哨

1938 年初，南京市民艰难地重建家园

1938 年，安全区内的难民在接受疫苗注射

兵显然不会说英文，只能说一点中文。搜查中，汤姆森博士用英文对哨兵说："我要把你的行为报告给日本大使馆。"这时，哨兵转过身，在他右脸颊上狠狠打了个耳光。

事发后，汤姆森到美国大使馆报告这起打耳光事件。阿利森随即陪同汤姆森去日本总领事馆提出强烈抗议，并要求一名日本官员和他们一起到事发地点，进行调查。然而，尽管阿利森一再敦促，在确凿的人证、物证面前，日军当局声称进行了彻底的调查，调查的结果显示哨兵没有打汤姆森的耳光，并要求对汤姆森给予"适当规劝"，同时威胁道，如果这样"侮辱日本士兵"的事件将来再度发生，日军当局将保留采取适当措施的权利。日军当局的态度似乎是对将来报告日本兵恶劣行径的任何美国人直接的威胁，也暗示日军有权管辖在中国的美国人。阿利森对这一粗暴结论大为不满，再一次提出了严正抗议。

阿利森还报告了南京居民反抗日军的统治。1938 年 7 月 26 日上午，有人将炸弹扔进市长办公室和老市政府办公地点。虽然没有造成严重损坏，也没有伤及高级官员，但是日军当局采取了严厉的措施封锁爆炸案件的消息，不让南京的老百姓得知。据传，有 9 名预谋此案的中国人被日军处决。7 月 29 日上午，从上海驶往南京的列车被游击队拦截了 20 多个小时，通往上海的铁路线因此中断。8 月 4 日，身份不明的中国爱国志士将手榴弹扔进鼓楼附近的日本宪兵队。据日本总领事说，有几个日本兵受了伤，但是来自中国人的消息称数名日军被炸死。据报道，在此之前的几个星期中，中国爱国志士经常枪击南京的日军哨兵。日军部队采取措施严加防范，使人相信即使在日军占领 7 个多月之后，南京城的老百姓仍没有顺从日本人的统治。

这些外交文件中，还留有一份南京大屠杀期间留在城里的外籍人士的名单。《南京美国财产与权益的状况》报告附件十五 A 列出在南京的 22 名外籍人士的姓名、国籍、工作单位。计有 14 名美国人，5 名德国人，1 位

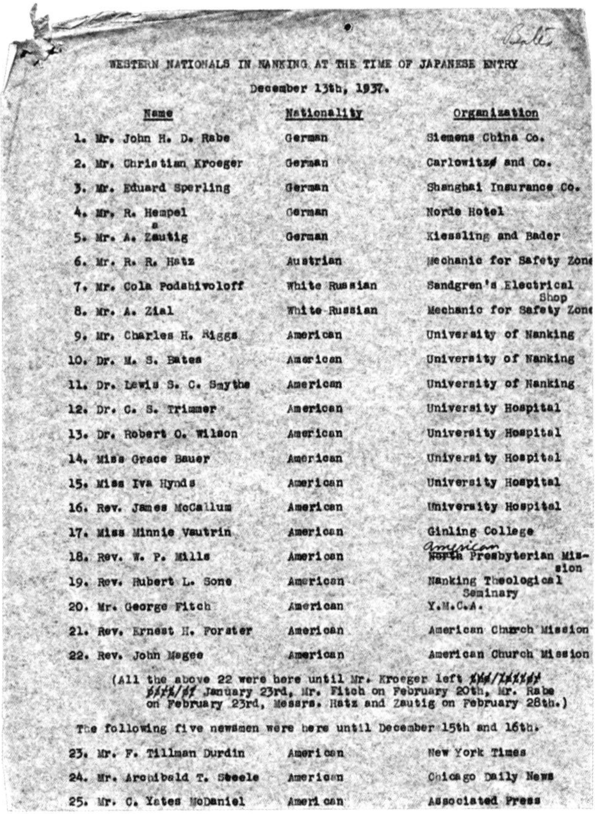

WESTERN NATIONALS IN NANKING AT THE TIME OF JAPANESE ENTRY

December 13th, 1937.

Name	Nationality	Organization
1. Mr. John H. D. Rabe	German	Siemens China Co.
2. Mr. Christian Kroeger	German	Carlowitz and Co.
3. Mr. Eduard Sperling	German	Shanghai Insurance Co.
4. Mr. R. Hempel	German	Nordic Hotel
5. Mr. A. Zautig	German	Kiessling and Bader
6. Mr. R. R. Hatz	Austrian	Mechanic for Safety Zone
7. Mr. Cola Podshivoloff	White Russian	Sandgren's Electrical Shop
8. Mr. A. Zial	White Russian	Mechanic for Safety Zone
9. Mr. Charles H. Riggs	American	University of Nanking
10. Dr. M. S. Bates	American	University of Nanking
11. Dr. Lewis S. C. Smythe	American	University of Nanking
12. Dr. C. S. Trimmer	American	University Hospital
13. Dr. Robert O. Wilson	American	University Hospital
14. Miss Grace Bauer	American	University Hospital
15. Miss Iva Hynds	American	University Hospital
16. Rev. James McCallum	American	University Hospital
17. Miss Minnie Vautrin	American	Ginling College
18. Rev. W. P. Mills	American	american ~~North~~ Presbyterian Mission
19. Rev. Hubert L. Sone	American	Nanking Theological Seminary
20. Mr. George Fitch	American	Y.M.C.A.
21. Rev. Ernest H. Forster	American	American Church Mission
22. Rev. John Magee	American	American Church Mission

(All the above 22 were here until Mr. Kroeger left January 23rd, Mr. Fitch on February 20th, Mr. Rabe on February 23rd, Messrs. Hatz and Zautig on February 28th.)

The following five newsmen were here until December 15th and 16th.

23. Mr. F. Tillman Durdin	American	New York Times
24. Mr. Archibald T. Steele	American	Chicago Daily News
25. Mr. C. Yates McDaniel	American	Associated Press

美国外交文件中关于日本人入侵时留在南京的西方人名单

奥地利人和 2 个白俄。这个名单为后人提供了当时在恐怖的环境中留在南京的外籍人员可靠准确的资料。

和美国传教士文献一样，美国外交文件以其第三方立场，在大屠杀事件发生当时，即已显现出无可替代的证明力。曾任日本外务省东亚事务局局长的石射猪太郎在东京审判时说，日军占领南京后，南京代理总领事福井淳从上海到任所后的第一份电报就是关于日军在南京的暴行的，该电报立即被送交陆军省军务局长。当时，外务大臣看到电报十分警觉和担忧，要他立即掩盖这些不体面的事情。后来，福井淳的书面报告送达，报告由南京的第三方人士用英语写成。外务大臣广田弘毅要求陆军大臣杉山就南京事态采取重大紧急举措。在接受质证时，石射猪太郎表示："我们把这些报告当作事实接受。"美国人士参与完成的报告被作为事实接受，说明美国文本在暴行发生时就让日方高层"发现"了南京大屠杀。而阿利森等外交官的特殊身份更是推动了南京大屠杀真相在国际上的传播。如果没有美国外交官的到来，身处南京的外籍证人就将继续处于孤立无援的状态；如果没有美国外交官的到来，包括马吉拍摄的原始视频资料在内的第一手资料就很难被带出南京；如果没有美国外交官与日军占领当局的反复交涉直至引发重大的"阿利森事件"，有恃无恐的日本侵略者也不会迫于外交压力而有所收敛。这些都是美国外交官阿利森所做出的无人可以替代的杰出贡献。

阿利森的在华外交活动对于美国政府改变对华策略起到了积极的作用。在中美外交官员的努力及美国总统罗斯福和美国财政部长摩根索的支持之下，1938 年底，美国给予中国 2500 万美元的桐油借款。桐油借款是继 1933 年棉麦借款后美国对中国的第一笔援助性贷款，其重要性在于，它标志着美国对东亚的外交政策有了微妙的转变。从此美国加大了援华抗战的力度，直至最终与中国结成反法西斯同盟。

余生浮沉

阿利森夫妇与印尼儿童

阿利森于1938年8月10日离开南京，回国休假。途中，在日本将1937年8月便从济南撤往东京的妻子珍妮特接上船。夫妇俩回到内布拉斯加，和他的双亲久别重逢的喜悦自不待言。1938年底，阿利森奉调到美国驻日本大阪总领事馆。

1942年12月8日上午7点，当阿利森起床时，得到了珍珠港事件爆发的消息。日本外务省一位名外交官向格鲁大使和全体美国外交官宣布了时任日本外相东乡茂德的信："谨通知阁下，自今日起，贵国与日本已进入战争状态。"于是乎，美国大使馆以及各领事馆职能就此停止。一切外交人员不得擅自离开使领馆，而与外部的一切联系也一律停止。外交人员及其家属将按照国际惯例予以保护并给予生活上的方便。阿利森和格鲁大使以及其他在日本的美国外交官一道被日方羁押了半年。1942年7月，日美双方通过中立国协商，最终在葡属东非（即今天莫桑比克首府马托普）交换了双方的外交人员及其家属。

从1942年至1945年，阿利森担任美国驻伦敦大使馆二等秘书，以后升任一等秘书。战后，他进入美国国务院，负责远东事务（1946—1948）。

阿利森主持的工作中，改造战后的日本是最重要的一项内容。战后初期，美国对日本政策的最终目标是使日本不再成为美国的威胁，并将其发展成按美国式民主原则运作的政府。在这个目标的导引下，以“民主化”“非军事化”“自由化”为中心的对日改造应运而生。应当说，美国对日本的改造，其初衷是符合时代潮流的，也符合战后世界人民对和平渴望的需求，当然，美国更多的是出于彻底摧毁日本战争能力的目的。

在美军占领日本本土尘埃落定的情况下，以远东军事法庭的审判为开端，拉开了清算日本战争责任的序幕。在政治上，美国占领当局要求日本政府保障公民言论和新闻自由；经济上，解散财阀、产出农业结构上的封建残余；思想上，要求日本政府清除极端民族主义和军国主义思想。1945 年 10 月 4 日，占领军当局发布指令废除限制思想、宗教信仰、集会、言论等自由的法令和规定。日本政府根据这一指令，废除了《治安维持法》《治安警察法》等有关法令。总体来说，通过占领和改造，美国取得了对日本灌输美国式的民主自由思想的胜利，而且这种改造还深入普通日本人的生活方式。

然而，随着朝鲜战争的爆发，日本在军事上、经济上和政治上对美国的意义日益显著，美国要使日本成为美国在远东地区遏制中国的后方基地，同时要让日本重整军备，以便美国腾出手来对付其他地区的“共产主义扩张”。朝鲜战争一爆发，以军需物资为中心的世界商品市场立即活跃，出现了所谓“动乱景气”。日本的出口也剧增，日本成了出兵朝鲜的美军基地，也是美国战斗部队的集结地、休养地。军需物资的大部分在日本筹集，武器的修理也在日本进行。具有生产大量军需经验的发达工业国日本很容易地就适应了美国的要求。

与此同时，美国还加紧了缔结对日和约的步伐。负责对日媾和事务的国务院顾问约翰·福斯特·杜勒斯(John Fotster Dulles)在战争爆发后即指出：“由于朝鲜战争的爆发，使对日和约变得更为重要而不是更不重要了。”阿利森在和日本谈判和平条约时担任杜勒斯的特别助手。在谈到对日媾和的基本原则时，杜勒斯明确指出对日和约必须要“确保日本附属世界自由国家，确保它在抵御共产党帝国主义进一步扩张中充分发挥作用。1951 年 9 月 8 日，美国单独与日本签订《旧金山合约》，日本被纳入美国“遏制”政策的轨道，成为美国在远东地区的反苏堡垒和军事基地。美日同盟的建立，实际上是美国对日本改造在国际局势影响下的美日关系发展而成的。

此后，阿利森还出任过负责远东事务的助理国务卿（1952—1953）。1952 年 10 月底，作为美国助理国务

1953年，阿利森就任美国驻日本大使

卿的阿利森访问台湾，要求蒋介石撤退缅北的国军残部，但遭到蒋介石的强烈反对。

1953年，阿利森出任美国驻日本大使，这也是他一生外交事业的顶点。

遗憾的是，由于冷战的加剧和国际外交格局的变化，美国对日本的政策逐步由清算转为扶植。作为驻日外交官，阿利森也必须为这一政策服务，一切不利于美日同盟构建的因素都被排除了。例如，阿利森等外交官1938年从南京发回美国国务院大量电报、文件。除了埃斯皮，1938年1月25日有关南京状况报告有一小部分在1946年东京远东国际军事法庭审判松井石根时作为控方证据在法庭上宣读，以及《美国外交关系》（1938年）第三卷、第四卷与《美国外交关系》（1931年至1941年）日本卷第一卷这三册在1955年出版时收录了一些阿利森的电报之外，这些涉及南京的电报均作为保密文件多年深藏在美国国务院的档案室中，从未面世。直到 20 世纪 70 年代中叶，这些文件解密之后移交给美国国家档案馆。

也正由于这些历史原因，曾经让美国人民极为同情、震惊和愤怒的南京大屠杀在冷战开始后，却从美国民众的视野中神秘地消失了。

这其中既有日本右翼势力对揭露南京大屠杀真相的阻挠，也有“受害者本身的沉默”，使亚洲以外的国家对南京大屠杀知之甚少。亲历南京大屠杀的美国传教士在回到美国后又遭审讯和隔离，身心遭受重创，大都过早地离开了人世。如，斯迈思博士于 1951 年离开金陵大学回国，贝德士则遭到拘留审查，马吉于 1953 年在美国去世。美国政府此时为获得日本的友谊和忠诚，不仅包庇了许多日本战犯，使他们重返政坛，还企图从公众意识中抹煞南京大屠杀。美国共和党参议员麦卡锡在 20 世纪 50 年代初掀起了反共反民主的政治迫害逆流，不仅使幸存的传教士三缄其口，而且专家学者也怕引火烧身，对南京大屠杀避而不谈。

在这样严酷的政治斗争环境下，阿利森的命运也遭受了重大挫折。1957—1958 年间，阿利森出任美国驻印度尼西亚大使。由于同情印尼总统苏加诺，阿利森和美国国务院决策层发生了龃龉，竟被后者贴上了“亲共分子”的标签。

早在艾森豪威尔上台前，亚非新兴国家的不结盟运动蓬勃发展，共产主义不断扩大在第三世界的影响力，成为美国政府必须面对的问题。在东南亚，尤其是在印度支那，中国对越南的援助引起了美国的担忧。对此，1952年6月出台的美国国家安全委员会文件指出，“无论东南亚任何国家由于共产党公开或者秘密的进攻而被共产党所控制，都将会产生致命的心理、政治和经济后果”。美国的目标应是“阻止东南亚国家华人共产党的

阿利森夫妇与印尼儿童

轨道，并协助它们提高从内外抵抗共产主义的能力和意志，以及推动对自由世界的巩固”。20世纪50年代中期，随着拉拢苏加诺政策的失败，美国政府转而支持反对苏加诺政权的“外岛叛乱”。

此时，新上任的美国驻印尼大使阿利森认为，反对苏加诺将引起苏加诺支持者的愤怒。1957年6月1日，阿利森在给国务院的一份电报中进一步表示，印尼现任内阁比前任采取了更加务实和建设性的方针，美国应当对这个新生的共和国保持耐心，不要怀疑印尼中央政府解决这些问题的能力。从阿利森的一系列电报可以看出，他认为印尼的叛乱只是中央政府遇到的暂时困难，其根源在于经济问题，美国应当对印尼中央政府保持信心并通过对外援助推动其稳定发展。

阿利森等人的观点与中央情报局的判断明显对立。有鉴于此，中央情报局希望向华盛顿高层证明叛乱已成定局，如此一来美国就没有理由反对对共产党持敌视态度的外岛武装势力，而支持一个日趋“被共产党控制的爪哇中央政府”。同时，为进一步获得华盛顿高层对干预“外岛叛乱”的支持，中央情报局甚至还制造舆论攻击阿利森所倡导的对印尼政策。1957年，从印尼考察归来的负责远东事务的中央情报局官员，向华盛顿方面报告，认为苏加诺已无法挽救局面，而阿利森大使则显得迷茫并且有同情共产主义的倾向。

很快，遭到政治打击的阿利森被调任美国驻捷克斯洛伐克大使（1958—1960），但在那里，他与美国国务院决策层的矛盾依然尖锐得无法调和。这也最终导致他在 1960 年 6 月离开外交界，到夏威夷大学任教。

1978 年 10 月 28 日，73 岁的阿利森在檀香山辞世。安葬于檀香山国立太平洋纪念公墓。

阿利森在南京时期的副手埃斯皮于 1938 年 6 月 3 日离开南京，奉调至驻广州总领事馆。1938 年底晋升为三等秘书，调任驻东京大使馆直至珍珠港事件爆发。他也和其他在日本的美国外交官一道被日本当局羁押了 6

阿利森夫妇墓碑

个月。此后 3 年，埃斯皮在美国驻中东的使领馆任职。1942 年 7 月在驻土耳其伊斯坦布尔总领事馆，同年 10 月调往驻埃及亚历山大港总领事馆。1943 年 4 月到驻开罗大使馆，并于 1944 年晋升为二等秘书。战后，他曾调回华盛顿在国务院任职。1948 年，调至驻玻利维亚拉巴斯大使馆任一等秘书。1951 年，任职驻奥地利维也纳大使馆。1952 年，为驻奥地利萨尔斯堡（Salzburg）领事。1953 年，为驻锡兰科伦坡大使馆公使。1956 年，任驻乌拉圭蒙得维的亚大使馆公使。埃斯皮于 1963 年退休。1976 年 1 月 27 日，在华盛顿特区逝世。

阿利森的另一名副手麦克法恩于 1938 年 3 月 13 日调回上海总领事馆。珍珠港事件后，他在上海和其他美国外交官一道被羁押了 6 个月。此后，他先后任职于美国驻乌拉圭蒙得维的亚大使馆（1942 年 9 月）、驻重庆大使馆（1943 年 10 月）、驻昆明总领事馆（1943 年 12 月），并晋升为副领事。战后，他辗转于世界各地的使领馆工作，包括驻上海总领事馆（1945 年 9 月）、驻天津总领事馆（1946 年 1 月）、驻爱尔兰都柏林大使馆（1946 年 9 月）和驻加拿大多伦多总领事馆（1949 年 2 月）。1950 年后，他曾一度回华盛顿任职于国务院。20 世纪 50 年代中叶，他的妻子及长子在几个月内先后去世使他倍受打击，几于精神崩溃，无法继续在外交界工作，病退离职。此后的三四十年间，他生活在社会的底层，靠打零工、杂活，诸如在餐馆厨房洗碗谋生。麦克法恩于2001年3月1日在纽约州的克林顿（Clinton）去世。

“青山遮不住，毕竟东流去。”随着冷战的结束和中美关系相对平稳的发展，南京大屠杀再次引起美国民众的关注。20世纪90年代以来，美国出版了大量关于日军慰安妇、活人医学试验、细菌和毒气战，以及南京大屠杀的小说、论文和著作。南京大屠杀时期留守传教士的信件、日记、笔记、照片等资料和美国外交档案的重新发现、整理和出版，客观公正地再现了当年日军的血腥暴行。美国人民为人类社会曾发生如此惨剧却毫不知情而气愤，更为日军惨绝人寰的大屠杀而震惊。今天的美国公众利用图书杂志、电影电视、互联网等各种途径，获得越来越多关于南京大屠杀的信息，对日本右翼分子竭力掩盖南京大屠杀真相的行径感到愤怒，要求政府向日本施加压力，迫使其承认战争中的暴行。

以阿利森、埃斯皮、麦克法恩为代表的美国外交官们在南京遏制侵华日军暴行、传播南京大屠杀事实真相的勇敢壮举，将永远彪炳史册！

主要参考资料 MAIN REFERENCES

1. 张宪文主编:《南京大屠杀史料集》4、6、63、69、70,江苏人民出版社、凤凰出版社 2005—2010 年版。

2. 张宪文、吕晶编:《见证与记录:南京大屠杀史料精选 西方史料》,江苏人民出版社 2014 年版。

3. 陆束屏编译:《南京大屠杀 英美人士的目击报道》,红旗出版社 1999 年版。

4. 张宪文主编:《南京大屠杀全史》,南京大学出版社 2012 年版。

5. 朱成山主编、陆束屏编译:《南京大屠杀史研究与文献 30·美国外交官的记载》,南京出版社 2012 年版。

6. 张生:《南京大屠杀史研究》,凤凰出版社 2012 年版。

7. 孙宅巍:《南京保卫战史》,南京出版社 2014 年版。

8.John Moore Allison, Ambassador from the Prairie Or, Allison Wonderland, Houghton Mifflin; First Edition edition (1973).

9.Suping Lu, They Were in Nanjing: The Nanjing Massacre Witnessed by American and British Nationals, Hong Kong University Press (December 7, 2004).